"What a great resource for anyone who respects the wisdom of Scripture and the practical knowledge that comes from counseling thousands of people. This is so easy to access that if you have a question about family, relationships, healing, emotions, and much more, you will most likely find it right here in *Live Right Now*."

—**Stephen Arterburn**, founder and chairman of
New Life Ministries, host of radio talk show
New Life Live and best-selling author

"*Live Right Now* is a resource for every woman who longs to find answers to perplexing questions about life, relationships, spiritual and emotional healing, parenting, financial matters, and so much more. Dr. Sabrina Black skillfully weaves practical information and biblical advice throughout each chapter in a way that leads the reader to the discovery of truth. I highly recommend this book!"

—**Carol Kent**, speaker and author of *Unquenchable:
Grow a Wildfire Faith that Will Endure Anything* and
When I Lay My Isaac Down

"When life's big issues come bearing down on you, it's hard to know where to find answers. That's the beauty of this book. *Live Right Now* is organized thematically to help you find solid, biblical answers to life's tough questions. It's ideal for personal application, group study, and as a trusted reference."

—**Steve Grissom**, founder of Church Initiative

"Sabrina Black writes from the perspective of woman of God who talks the talk and walks the walk. I strongly endorse her as a counselor and as a friend. In *Live Right Now*, her responses to some of life's toughest questions are culturally relevant, psychologically sound, and grounded in God's Word."

—**Rev. Mark Crear**, PhD, BCPCC

"Sabrina Black is one of the most compassionate and critical thinkers I have ever encountered. Her wit and wisdom pour through on every page of this amazing book. If you have seen your dreams and passion die due to sin, setbacks, or strongholds, it's time to 'live right now'!"

—**Chris Brooks**, campus dean,
Moody Theological Seminary—Michigan

"Whenever I encounter a gift, I acknowledge it. In her latest book, *Live Right Now*, Dr. Sabrina Black gives us a gift. She not only responds to questions with sound biblical answers, but she also helps her readers to stand and to find their own voices. She unashamedly shines a light in darkness and helps them to see that God had not abandoned them—He is still ever-present and still speaking through His Word."

—**Dr. Gail Hayes**, author of
The Power of a Woman Who Leads

LIVE RIGHT NOW

HONEST ANSWERS TO LIFE'S TOUGH QUESTIONS

DR. SABRINA BLACK

DISCOVERY HOUSE
PUBLISHERS®

ISBN 978-1- 57293-816-8

Printed in the United States of America

First printing in 2014

In memory of

Adell Berniece Oaks Miree
My grandmother, a woman of ancient wit and wisdom.
She taught us that "your folks are your folks"
and "love is love."
She gave birth to seventeen children
who have continued to be fruitful
and raise generations in the fear of the Lord.
She died on December 19, 1981, three years after her
fiftieth wedding anniversary.

and

Dear Abby
A woman whose column I read for years
and whom I admired from afar.
I often wondered how I would respond
to the people who wrote in.
She died on January 17, 2013, just as I was
completing this book.

CONTENTS

INTRODUCTION

Do you know who your true friends are? Do you know what a true friend is? Who can you call in distress? Who can you cry with? Who will encourage you? Who will help you forget your problems? Who will help you live life in spite of your problems?

But just as importantly: who will challenge you?

I am that friend. People know to call me when they are ready to live right. When they are ready to pick up their mat and walk. People come to me when they are done making excuses and blame-shifting. I help people who are ready to take ownership of their lives, the choices they are making, and how they respond to the things they cannot control. When you are ready to live right, I am the person who will help you with the difficult decisions.

It would sure be nice to have someone tell you to comb your hair before you took an important photo or went on television; or that a certain shade of green looked more like puke than grass. Wouldn't it be great to have someone care enough to tell you the truth about a bad relationship? To have someone not only tell you about your life issues, but help you work through them? Wouldn't it be nice to also have someone remind you of the difference between right and wrong, according to God's Word?

One of my favorite classic movie phrases is, "You can't handle the truth!" When Jack Nicholson made that statement from the witness stand in *A Few Good Men*, he was furious because he was being challenged to tell the truth. His retort implied the prosecuting attorney and everyone else in the room would rather be lied to than forced to deal with the plain truth that made up the realities of their lives. Think about how often in the last twenty-four hours the plain truth appeared dressed up and camouflaged to the point of being incognito. Most of you have heard it or at least thought about it at some point when you struggled to share the truth others would rather not hear.

As Christians, we should desire the truth in all things—especially in our hearts. In spite of this, we lie to others and even, subconsciously, to ourselves.

The apostle Paul is transparent about his own struggles in Romans 7. He suggests the good he would do he does not do and the evil he knows not to do he continues to find himself doing. He asks a critical question: "Who will deliver me from this body of death?" The answer: "Thanks be to God through Christ Jesus!"

The truth Paul knew then is still relevant today. Through the Word of God and our relationship with Christ, we gain strength to overcome the battle within and to do right in the midst of a world where people are doing wrong.

The world reinforces and glorifies wrong actions, wrong choices, and wrong thoughts. If we let the world impact our thinking, we will give in to the desires of our flesh. You may remember the world's hedonistic philosophy: "If it feels good, do it." This mind-set feeds the flesh, perpetuates the lies of the enemy, and leads to wrong living.

When you are ready to live right, you must turn away from the world's system—no matter how good it may feel or convincing it sounds. It does not even matter if you think everyone else is doing it (which you will find is most often a lie).

We are living in a time when many people no longer listen to or endure sound doctrine. They would rather hear things to satisfy the desires of their flesh. They would rather believe a lie than recognize the truth according to the Word of God. Consider the words found in Isaiah 30:10: "They say to the seers, 'See no more visions!' and to the prophets, 'Give us no more visions of what is right! Tell us pleasant things, prophesy illusions'" (NIV).

In other words, "lie to us."

The world conditions us to become unintentional liars. We lie to others and ourselves because it makes us feel good. The lies we believe impact our spiritual growth, interfere with our intimacy in relationships, and impede our leadership.

We should not become like the people mentioned in 2 Timothy 4:3: "For a time is coming, when people will no longer listen to sound and wholesome teaching. They will follow their own desires and will look for teachers who will tell them whatever their itching ears want to hear" (NLT). Instead, consider the plain truth found in the Word of God, which tells us in Genesis 4:7: "If you do what is right, will you not be accepted?" (NIV). Jeremiah 29:11 tells us God knows the plans He has for us, the promises He has given to us, and the timing things will be revealed to us.

Consider taking this simple test. Listen for and tell only the plain truth to yourself and to others for the next twenty-four hours, and then meditate on what God is speaking to you. It sounds easy, but we are so accustomed to embellishing the truth, framing the truth, and skewing the truth, we no longer realize we are lying. Lying has become our way of telling what we have convinced ourselves is the truth. Sometimes we color the truth so much, it is no longer even a shade of the original.

This book is based on the truth of God's Word. It is straight talk, and it is "naked truth." We are bare before God; He sees all. God wants us to be honest with ourselves, honest in our dealings, and honest in our hearts. When obedience to God's Word is practiced, we experience the fruit of the Spirit proclaimed in Galatians 5:22–23—the true love, joy, and peace that eludes so many.

This book is a topical compilation of real questions by real people—people who have struggles with which you just may be familiar! If you use it in a group study, you can create a "mutual accountability" group to help all of you stay on course. Sharing your growth in a supportive community as you embrace and/or wrestle with the answers given in each scenario will help you to grapple with your own situations. You may also discover God's Word of truth lives in you—waiting to be drawn out and applied to real-life situations. Consider what you would tell the person in the stories you will read and what you would want someone to tell you if you were that person. Consider what a difference it would make in our homes, churches, and communities if we began to more consistently and intentionally live guided by God's truth and encourage others to do the same.

We need to shake the people of God and wake them up so they no longer slumber and sleep with the enemy. If we continue to believe lies even when confronted with God's truth, the enemy will creep into our lives and establish a foothold. There is a great need for someone to tell the truth and expose the lies and deceptions we live with daily. This book is designed to take you into the heart of God's truth.

I am the friend you call when you are ready to live right. It has been my discovery over the years when people who would normally exercise good common sense, practical wisdom, and godly behavior make questionable choices, it is because they are usually under some pressure from an external source or external locust of control. It is the "evil we know not to do."

There are times in all of our lives when we stop and ask ourselves the "what if?" questions. Most of us resolve that the question is not worth entertaining. We may laugh at ourselves, shrug, and keep going. However, there are people who struggle with "the good they know to do, yet they don't do."

There are also those who really think they are doing right, but have been exposed to subtle or even blatant false teachings. These people struggle with the idea of doing wrong when they have followed what they have been taught. They want to live right, but they have done wrong because they were led astray by someone else's wrongdoing. Whether you have not been living right based on your own choices—or because someone else deceived you—it is time to get back on the path of righteousness.

It is my prayer that you are already living right and just need a few answers for life's tough questions. This is the time to challenge yourself—and those around you—to stop accepting the ways of the world and live the truth of God's Word. *Live Right Now* will help you and the people in your circle get excited about living guided by God's truth. My goal is to help you become equipped and empowered to live according to the Word of God and thereby enhance your life.

The transformation in your life from being in the presence of the Lord and applying the Bible will display the intimacy of your relationship with God for others to see.

Whatever you are fighting to overcome right now, you have been in it already far too long. I have always been a bottom line, no nonsense person. So when I counsel in my practice, I bring a sense of urgency. Why wait another week, day, or hour to address what you know to be an issue impacting the state of your emotions, relationships, and spiritual growth? I am often reminded about the story of Pharaoh and Moses in the eighth chapter of the book of Exodus. Pharaoh was given an opportunity to change his situation and circumstance at any time and he chose tomorrow, rather than today. Don't wait! Decide today you want to become more like Christ in your daily walk. Decide today you want to be strengthened in your resolve to live right.

> *Decide today you want to become more like Christ in your daily walk. Decide today you want to be strengthened in your resolve to live right.*

I speak from a heart of love and a strong desire to see people live the abundant life God promises in John 10:10. Overcoming whatever battle you are fighting in your life right now requires a sense of urgency. Honestly, you have probably been fighting far too long. When you consider every good and perfect gift God has for you and the life He died for you to live, you should be compelled to stop wasting time and live life to the fullest. Join me on this journey to live right now!

When you are ready to live right, you will study the Word of God. Then, you will let God's Word influence your thinking. When godly thoughts impact the way you live your life, you can live, share, and defend our faith. We study the Word of God to understand how to apply it in our lives. We share God's Word to help others live right and to reinforce what we know. It is a blessing to hear yourself proclaim the Word of God. It is affirmation that you have successfully hidden the Word of God in your heart so you will not sin against Him. With the plain truth of God's Word guiding your heart, you can encourage others to not sin against God by following the ways of the world. When you study the Word of God, you can defend your faith against foolishness, wickedness, old wives' tales, and societal propaganda.

Are you ready to live right? Now?

CHAPTER 1

RELATIONSHIPS

What counts in making a happy marriage is not so much how compatible you are, but how you deal with incompatibility.

Leo Tolstoy

"A new commandment I give unto you, that ye love one another; as I have loved you, that ye also love one another."

John 13:34 (KJV)

I remember the first time I heard someone say, "Oh, I love God; it's His people I have a hard time with." It baffled me. Were they serious? I heard it again and again. The Bible asks the question in 1 John 4:20, "for he who does not love his brother whom he has seen, how can he love God whom he has not seen?" (NKJV). If we do this, the Bible says we are liars. That may sound harsh, but it is the key relationship question we must ask ourselves.

We serve a relational God who wants us to be in right relationship with Him and with one another. The intensity and intimacy of our vertical relationship with God greatly impacts our ability to engage, maintain, and sustain our horizontal relationship with others. When we feel loved by God—valued and significant—we can embrace others.

> **Relationships are not just about you, but what God is doing in you and through you for others.**

Too often, we avoid people and withdraw ourselves from the company of those who challenge us. Instead, I challenge you to risk entering into relationship with Christlike vulnerability. People are important to God. Just as He loves you, God also loves others. People are lovable, forgivable, valuable, and changeable—not by us, but by the Lord. He is still in the process of perfecting us all.

Relationships are not just about you, but what God is doing in you and through you for others.

We are bombarded daily by the world's view on relationships. "Lies are the only things that keep couples together." "Good sex is the only way to have a good relationship." "You are the most important person in any relationship." Books, movies, and talk shows reinforce these ideas by providing false evidence to support them. However, according to Scripture we are living epistles, and others are reading our lives. We therefore become the model of how to live effectively in relationships. But how do we become the models God is calling us to be?

God promises in James 4:8, "Draw near to God and He will draw near to you." He calls us to abide in Him and He will abide in us in John 15:4. The first commandment is to love God, and then to love others as we love ourselves (Mark 12:28–31). The most effective Christian models of godly relationships get the vertical part right first.

But no man is an island; we need each other. We are interdependent and cannot be a fully developed human being without interacting with others. There is an important progression to consider, and that is the progression from family to the church to the world. The order is important: to engage in godly relationships with believers is useless if you have not tackled the challenge of living in a family structure. Then, once we have matured in our relationships with believers, we can confidently face those in the world, whose views and values may be different from ours, with love and compassion. There are so many different types of relationships: spouses, friends, neighbors, coworkers, parent/child, employee/employer, and many more. Each of these relationships gives us an opportunity to demonstrate godly living by applying Scripture to every situation we encounter. Consider how many of these verses you live daily and research others as you have time. Investing in this study will improve the quality of all your relationships:

Love one another	John 13:34, 35
Build up one another	Romans 14:19
Be kind to one another	Ephesians 4:32
Be at peace with one another	Mark 9:50
Admonish one another	Romans 15:14
Bear one another's burdens	Galatians 6:2
Comfort one another	1 Thessalonians 4:18
Forgive each other	Ephesians 4:32
Confess your sins to one another	James 5:16
Show hospitality to one another	1 Peter 4:9
Give preference to one another	Romans 12:10
Speak to one another in psalms and hymns	Ephesians 5:19

Encourage one another	1 Thessalonians 5:11
Pray for one another	James 5:16
Have fellowship with one another	1 John 1:7
Spur one another on to love and good deeds	Hebrews 10:24
Do not slander one another	James 4:11
Do not grumble against one another	James 5:9
Live in harmony with one another	1 Peter 3:8
Lay down your life for one another	1 John 3:16–18
Restore one another	Galatians 6:1–3
Bear with one another	Colossians 3:12–14
Do not lie to one another	Colossians 3:9
Disciple and teach one another	2 Timothy 2:2
Please one another	Romans 15:2
Accept one another	Romans 15:7
Suffer with one another	1 Corinthians 12:26
Rejoice with one another	Romans 12:15
Honor one another	Romans 12:10

God's Word abounds with truth and gives us instructions or guidelines of how we should relate one to another. Making and maintaining right relationships is symbolic of our level of spiritual growth. When we live God's Word, we enjoy the relationships God chooses for us and avoid toxic unhealthy relationships. These Scriptures can be a checklist for your relationships.

Where do you need growth? Which of your relationships could be transformed immediately if you applied Scripture to your behavior and interaction?

- Marriage and In-Laws
- Dating

- Friends
- Co-Workers
- Caregiving
- Mentoring and Discipleship

Now, let's take a look at some real-life scenarios. Maybe you will find yourself in these; if you do, counsel yourself. Maybe you will find that these scenarios remind you of others; if you do, you now have information to help them.

Q: I'm 40 years old and my life is a lie. I have what many consider the perfect lifestyle. I have two kids (boy and girl), the big house with the white picket fence, and I'm a stay-at-home mom with a husband who makes over six figures. I have an eight-carat diamond solitaire ring along with all the high fashion shoes, bags, and clothes. In addition, my husband is the perfect father and my family adores him. However, my husband is a serial cheater. I spend most of my nights alone in my big house with my two kids while my husband travels the country claiming that he is working hard to keep his family in this lifestyle. I still love him with all my heart and I've given up my life for this man. I trusted him with our future and depended on him to love and adore me our entire life. I know God is aware of my burdens, but I'm afraid to confess them aloud. For some silly reason I feel if I say them aloud, then I will have to face them and admit that I know what he's doing. I know this sounds crazy, but it's the truth! Can I pray to God for deliverance from this love that I have for him in order to release myself from the burden and falsehood of this lifestyle? Signed: Matthew 6:6

A: Dear Matthew 6:6,

God is love. He will never deliver you from love, but He has already provided deliverance from an adulterous spouse. When a spouse breaks the marriage vows, you are free to stay and forgive your spouse or you are free to leave. This is because your spouse has broken covenant with you.

I am glad you know this is not a perfect lifestyle. You have many wonderful things in your life. Some of them are gifts from God and some are the trappings of the world. Your children, your health, your knowledge of God's love, and the power of prayer are all gifts from God. On the other hand, the eight-carat diamond solitaire ring, along with all the high fashion shoes, bags, and clothes you could ever want, appear to be a trap your husband has set to hold you captive, silent, and alone.

You don't have to confess your husband's sins aloud to face them; you are already facing them, and their consequences. You speak of your husband as a serial cheater, which means you know he will continue his cheating ways, just like a serial killer who will not stop until caught and brought to justice.

God gives you the ability to confront and forgive your husband. Who knows, maybe he will admit, confess, and repent of his sins. If he does not, you have a choice to make—you can stay and carry the burden and falsehood of your present lifestyle or you can walk away and build a God-honoring lifestyle based on love and truth for you and your children.

Q: My husband and I are both saved. I am young, sexy, pretty, and intelligent. I am also a good wife; so why did my husband cheat on me? I can't imagine what I did wrong. Yet somehow I'm wondering, "Whose fault is it?" He is the one that cheated so why do I feel so guilty, embarrassed, and ashamed? He is involved with a woman on his job; he doesn't know that I am aware of what is going on. I believe he loves me and is just having a fling. I am willing to forgive him even before he asks me to, and I know he will when he finds out I know. My problem is I want to get even with him before I tell him I know. Should we stay together? What about diseases? Will he ever change? This has happened more than once. I am daydreaming about having an affair. Then we can forgive each other. Should I trust him again? Signed: Why Must We Cheat? or Two Can Play That Game!

A: Dear Why Must We Cheat? or Two Can Play That Game!

You must let go of any desire for revenge. Furthermore, stop daydreaming about having an affair right now! That is not an option. It helps that you are willing to forgive, because adultery does not have to lead to divorce. Couples can recover after an affair.

Infidelity studies show numerous reasons why men/women cheat. I'm sure you can identify a few reasons of your own. However for me, sin continues to be the problem plaguing us most often when we look at the issues of life. First Corinthians 7:2 (KJV) says, "Nevertheless, to avoid fornication, let every man have his own wife, and let every woman have her own husband" (KJV). First Thessalonians 4:3–5 says,

"For this is the will of God, even your sanctification that ye should abstain from fornication. That every one of you should know how to possess his vessel in sanctification and honour; not in the lust of concupiscence, even as the Gentiles which know not God" (KJV).

When you are faced with adultery, dealing with your emotional roller coaster will be one of the greatest challenges. Even beyond the decision to trust your spouse again, is the decision to trust God with your emotions. Psychologically the person whose trust has been betrayed will often feel depression, anxiety, anger, grief, and loss. Adultery is an indication something is wrong at a much deeper level. When a man cheats, it is not only against his wife, but he has acted contrary to his conscience and his heart has strayed from God.

Your marriage is not a game. Don't begin to play with your emotions, your affections, or your body. Your husband has already played enough. The reality of sin is not make-believe. Stop pretending and approach your husband. If you know he loves you, don't sit around waiting on him to find out you know about his affair. Bring it up as a matter of concern. Since both of you are saved, the conversation should focus more on sinning against God. Your marriage should be holy ground and a representation of Christ's love. I don't know how the matter was addressed the first time, but this time, you should seek outside help from a professional Christian counselor or pastor.

Q: I married a good Christian man and looked forward to a life of joy and happiness ever after. I had a wonderful sense of security because I thought I was in a lifelong relationship with this man. I thought we would be together forever. I thought we were both happy, but then two years into our marriage things started to change. He started spending more time with his friends. Now he has even stopped attending church with me, reading the Bible, and praying with me. These changes are so unlike him. He is acting suspicious and has stopped answering his cell phone around me. I am worried that he is being unfaithful to me. When I asked him about the calls, he started finding fault with me and refused to answer me. A few days later my friend told me he was cheating. She said she could prove what I already knew to be true. I am devastated. Signed: Why Do Christian Men Cheat? And What Am I to Do Now?

A: Dear Why Do Christian Men Cheat? And What Am I to Do Now?

Those are both good questions! Let's start with the first one. The responses are as vast as the people you ask. You have heard it said before, if you ask twenty people you will get twenty different answers. Well, I prayed about whom to ask between men and women knowing that their answers would vary. I opted to poll the gender in question. So, I asked men who only identified themselves as Christians and men from different denominations. Christian men who will not be faithful continue to pose a growing problem for lasting relationships.

It can be shocking for a woman when she discovers her spouse is cheating even though she may have seen the signs of infidelity for months. Even more shocking is learning that other Christian women are facing the same heartbreak. Often many among their circle of friends have lived through similar situations. Before we look at the men's responses, let's make sure we have the same understanding of what it means to cheat, have an affair, commit adultery, or sin against God, your body, and your spouse. Here are a few definitions:

- Sexual behavior desired or realized outside of the confines of marriage.
- A sexual liaison outside of the marriage relationship.
- A violation of God's holy ordinance concerning marriage.
- A voluntary sexual act between a man/woman and someone other than his/her spouse.
- Non-sexual behavior that involves sharing intimate feelings and thoughts with an extramarital partner or secrecy that violates trust.
- Sexual behavior outside of the marriage that violates the explicit or implicit expectations of the relationship.
- Lack of sexual boundaries and regard for intimacy.
- An amorous relationship between two people who are not married to each other.

Here are the top twelve reasons men gave me for why they cheat. These responses were from men in four different denominations.

1. Sin nature.
2. Lack of self-control.
3. Christian women change.
4. Same reason as other men.
5. Pressures of work.

6. Sexually explicit material all around them.

7. Women make it easy for them.

8. They want to have their cake and eat it too.

9. Boredom.

10. In need of a conquest.

11. Forbidden fruit.

12. Lonely at home / unmet emotional needs.

Sometimes knowing why is helpful; other times it still makes no sense at all. And now your second question: What can you do about it? There is nothing you can do about his choices. God will hold him accountable. But there is something you can do about your responses. Pray! Pray for God to move him to repentance and convict him regarding sin. Pray for the Lord to keep you and your husband safe from disease. Pray your husband is willing to seek counseling and stay the course of recovery. Pray that the two of you are able to work together on forgiveness. Pray.

Also, you must protect yourself. Since your husband has decided to be unfaithful, you should insist on him wearing a condom every time you have sexual relations—and you should explain why. Who knows? That just might make him wake up!

Q: Before becoming Christians my husband and I were both unfaithful. We have hurt each other but still want to work it out. Will counseling help us? How can couples recover? Can a marriage relationship be healed that has been shattered by adultery? Can couples rebuild broken vows after an affair? Signed: Please Say There Is Still Hope

A: Dear Please Say There Is Still Hope,

Absolutely! There is hope. Healing is a process that takes time and willingness on the part of both individuals. The process of rebuilding and reconciliation include three key components: repentance, forgiveness and restoration. How do we rebuild broken vows after an affair? After years of experience helping couples work through issues of adultery and rebuild their marriage, I have developed a three-stage integrative model based on Hope, Help, and Healing.

I am encouraged the two of you want to work it out. If your husband is willing to seek counseling, then I would suggest finding a Christian counselor who can walk with the two of you through the process. But don't wait. You can begin with the stages below.

Stage 1: HOPE (1 Corinthians 10:13)

In the first stage, hurting and unfaithful partners are directed to make sense out of the avalanche of emotions released by the adultery. This will give them a sense of balance so they will not feel they are crazy, hopeless, or alone. Key areas of focus include:

- Hope to survive the trauma.
- Hope that the relationship can be transformed.
- Hope that God is working in the midst of the situation.

Stage 2: HELP (Psalm 46:1; Isaiah 61:1–4)

In the second stage, partners are coached to make a biblical—not emotional—decision to recommit to the marriage.

They are encouraged to explore their ambivalence about their relationship, develop a realistic yet biblical concept of love, and take responsibility for how their early experiences compromised their ability to be intimate and faithful in this relationship. Key areas of focus include:

- Help sorting out your emotions.
- Help seeking God's will.
- Help working through the process of pain (adultery hurts).

Stage 3: HEALING (Ephesians 4:22–24)

In the third stage, a road map is provided for rebuilding trust and intimacy, and learning to forgive. Marriage partners are encouraged to focus on personal growth as a result of the experience.

- Healing in the area of forgiveness.
- Healing in the area of trust and intimacy.
- Healing in the area of love according to God's Word.

In conjunction with this integrative model is the need to restore the soul and renew the mind—following the biblical theme that reconciliation to God precedes restoration with one another. This model mandates obedience to the Word. What God hath joined together . . . let no one separate, even the two of you. Remember God is faithful; hope is possible.

Q: I'm a 37-year-old woman; I have been with my boyfriend for over five years. He is much older, twenty years my senior.

I don't have any children, but he does from his previous marriage. I truly love this man. I attend church almost every Sunday and Bible study when I can. My boyfriend doesn't want to get married again and has never told me he loves me—only that he cares deeply. I do not want any children due to the fear I may turn out like my mother, with whom I no longer have contact. My boyfriend doesn't attend church but believes in God. He is a wonderful man, and I appreciate him being a part of my life in so many ways. I've received advice from various individuals in my life, ranging in age, about this type of relationship with all of them saying the same thing: "There is no future for you with him." My passion for Christ has grown so much over the past year I now find myself at the crossroads with what's right in God's eyes. I hear so many stories of other women with justifiable reasons to leave their relationships, but still they stay. Other than what I've mentioned, my boyfriend is a very good man. I know all things are possible with Christ, but this man is dead-set on not remarrying or saying the words "I love you." Signed: Can I Keep Him Please?

A: Dear Can I Keep Him Please?

The answer is no, no-no, no, not as a boyfriend, unless you are a glutton for punishment. If you are saved, the only relationship you can have with this man is friendship—and that without benefits. I am not trying to be harsh; I just see too many red flags, which mean stop before you get hurt. Clearly you have concerns. If you thought it was permissible to keep him, you would not be asking questions.

How many people need to tell you no before you get the message? First, he is too old for you; when you are 62 he will be 82, if he is blessed with extra strength. Second, do you ever want to marry? He never wants to marry again. You have already held on five years. He has not changed his mind. Do you want to sacrifice another five years of your life waiting? Third, you love him and he cares for you—how do you feel about that? Do you ever long to be loved, or is his care sufficient? Finally, he has children, and you say you don't want any; someday that may change. If it does, he may be too old to have any children and you still won't be married.

Now that you are at the crossroads and want to do right in God's eyes, unless you can have a sexless friendship with this man, you are headed for heartbreak. As wonderful as you say he is, he is still dead-set on not remarrying or saying the words "I love you." It doesn't matter what other women are doing. Don't run past the red flags. You already know in your heart you held onto him too long. Hear this as confirmation and a final word of instruction: Let him go; there is no future there.

Q: I'm 30 years old and I feel discouraged with God because I still haven't received an answer to my question concerning the continuation of my marriage. I'm in love with another man, and I want to be with him. I do not want my current husband anymore. Neither my husband nor I have cheated. What can I do! I understand that a delay doesn't mean it's a denial. I really need an answer. I can't live like this anymore! I'm very unhappy. I'm in love with another man. I keep reminding myself of Hebrews 10:36–37 but nothing has changed. Signed: Pilot Marriage

A: Dear Pilot Marriage,

Well, that's a misnomer. Marriage is a covenant between the two of you, honored and sanctioned by God. Feeling discouraged is nothing new and certainly not a reason for wandering or divorce. Discouragement is not from God, but a trick of the enemy to cause you to question God's faithfulness in taking care of your needs.

You say you are 30 years old, but you sound more like a spoiled two-year-old. "I don't want the red lollipop anymore; I want the orange one; it looks better. I don't want my current husband; I want another one." You are not waiting on God; you are looking for a way to justify your behavior. God has not kept you waiting; your answer has been in your Bible all the time. Read Genesis 2:20–24. God has answered; are you listening? Will you hear and obey?

God never intended for marriage to be a ninety-day option, but a lifetime commitment. There is no test drive, trial period, warranty rebates, refunds, or exchanges on your mate in marriage. Once you say, "I do," it's done.

How did you fall in love with another man and believe you are still faithful? Your affections are sorely misplaced; you are unfaithful in your heart. Love God enough to not violate His Word or yourself. God can renew, restore, or bring forth love from you toward your husband. I encourage you to cut off all ties with this other man before you go any further. Start rebuilding your marriage. Don't allow inordinate affections to lead you further on the path to fornication and adultery. What can you do? Repent. Guard your heart with all diligence. Ask God to show you what voids in your life need to be filled, and then let God fill them.

"For ye have need of patience, that, after ye have done the will of God, ye might receive the promise. For yet a little while, and he that shall come will come, and will not tarry" (Hebrews 10:36–37 KJV). You have need of patience while you work on your marriage, and nothing is going to change until you do. Doing wrong will only provide temporary happiness and much conflict. Remember, lasting joy is the by-product of obeying God.

Q: I have been dating this guy for several months and we have really been enjoying each other. So much so that I believe I may need to broach a sensitive subject with him before we go any further in the relationship. I had a serious illness three years ago that caused me to have a hysterectomy. I had not brought this up to him before because I figured it was too early in the relationship. He is the first guy I have been serious about since my surgery. I don't want to lose him but I feel like I am being deceitful the longer I go without telling him. How should I bring up this issue to him? I will never be able to have children. Our relationship has been like the perfect dream and I don't want to wake up. Signed: Sleeping Beauty

A: Dear Sleeping Beauty,

I am glad to report that life can be like a dream even when we are awake. Wake up, Sleeping Beauty; if you think he may be the one, you owe him the truth. It would be deceitful not to tell him, because he seems to be enjoying the relationship as well. If you lose him, he was not the one. Better to find out now than later. I know it will hurt now, but it will hurt even worse when you are more involved in the relationship. There is only one way to do this—just tell him the truth. And you can still have children. There are so many options open to women who cannot carry a child themselves. Wake up and check them out, and be prepared to discuss them with your friend with whom you believe there may be a future.

Q: I have been married for ten years. I have a wonderful husband and all that any woman could ever want in a marriage. But I cheat! I've never been able to be faithful to a man. I've also had counseling and it helped for one year, and then I was back to doing what I know best—cheating! I don't want to divorce my husband because I truly love him with all my heart, but I'm always finding myself needing more. I love the thrill and excitement a new lover brings; it is like a new car, new shoes, or jewelry. I have all I need in life; still I lust for more. Signed: Lusting for More

A: Dear Lusting for More,

Do you really know what love is? Just keep it up, and you will end up with nothing. All the things you identified are temporal, yet I hear a deeper longing in your soul. It appears you are attempting to fill a void in your life by reaching for what does not satisfy. Are you a Christian? If not, nothing will ever satisfy you for long and you will not find true contentment until you find rest in God.

Your situation brings to remembrance the woman at the well (John 4:1–30, 39–42). Her story speaks to the grace, love, and forgiveness of God. I would encourage you to study the following Scriptures:

- Let us behave properly as in the day, not in carousing and drunkenness, not in sexual promiscuity and sensuality, not in strife and jealousy. But put on the Lord Jesus Christ, and make no provision for the flesh in regard to its lusts. Romans 13:13–14

- Everyone who practices sin also practices lawlessness; and sin is lawlessness. 1 John 3:4

- Do not love the world, nor the things in the world. If anyone loves the world, the love of the Father is not in him. For all that is in the world, the lust of the flesh and the lust of the eyes and the boastful pride of life, is not from the Father, but is from the world. 1 John 2:15–16

- And do not lead us into temptation, but deliver us from evil. Matthew 6:13

Seek Christian counseling to help you get to the root of your sins and transform your life. If you are a Christian, you know the error and folly of your behavior. Remember God is not mocked. I pray you repent before God's judgment falls heavily upon you.

Q: I'm a 37-year old woman who has lost faith in finding true love. I've done everything God asked me to do, but still I'm alone. I'm not the kind of woman who looks for love. I remained abstinent until marriage. I waited on God to show me the way. I waited for the right man. I felt one man was the right one for me (heaven sent), but he wasn't. He betrayed me. He became distant and often left home for long hours without any explanation. I recently learned he has been sleeping around. I'm very hurt and bitter; I'm heartbroken and it's hard for me to see past the pain. Signed: Sent from Heaven; Took Me Through Hell

A: Dear Sent from Heaven; Took Me Through Hell,

I started to pray for you as I read your letter. You sound emotionally broken. I can imagine and certainly understand how you must feel. It is devastating to feel God has let you down. Please believe me when I tell you God is faithful and always fulfills His promises to us. He will never let you down. The problem is not with God; it is with people. We believe God owes us because we have done everything He asked us to do.

Why did you think this man was sent from heaven? Did he take you through hell or did you allow yourself to go just to be with him? Were there signals along the way warning you this relationship was heading in the wrong direction? We will miss the signs when we think, "God has to send me a good man because I have been such a good woman."

Be encouraged, my sister. Use this time to get to know God better. I know you are very hurt and bitter right now, but remember, a man betrayed you—not God. Turn to God, cry out to Him, and pour out your pain and disappointments before Him. You will find Him waiting to heal your broken heart and mend your wounded spirit.

You are not the first woman who has been betrayed. Bitterness will keep you in bondage and lead to further betrayal in future relationships. Dig up every root of bitterness. Seek biblical counsel to help you work through issues of forgiveness. Follow the example of the One who was truly sent from heaven. Jesus prayed to God to forgive those who betrayed

Him. Continue to be the kind of woman who waits on God to show you the way.

Q: I recently found out that my dad has another daughter attending the same university as my older sister. My mother is always preaching about the goodness of a godly man and how her husband is the best among the brothers in our national denomination. Should I share my father's double life with my mother? I do not want to hurt her, but I also do not want her to continue to believe my father's lies. Signed: Ready to Tell

A: Dear Ready to Tell,

If your mother chooses to see her husband's goodness, why would you want to break up your mother's home, destroy her dream, or bring up the truth she may already know? How do you know your father is lying and has a double life, if you just recently found out about your other sister? This may be an incident your mother and father have dealt with, not a lifestyle. Your mother has been with your father a long time. She sees her husband as the best among the brothers in her national denomination. I would rather believe his lifestyle is based on their years together—not an incident that happened many years ago. Remember the goal of love is to cover and protect, not uncover and reveal.

Everything you know does not need to be told nor is it yours to tell. In some situations you should tell, and in others . . . maybe not. It depends on the person and their relationship. If this was a baby, maybe my advice would be different, but she is already in college. Who will you help by telling your mother? You say you don't want to hurt your mother. Then don't! If you desire a relationship with this sister, then pray before you proceed. Her life may also be turned upside down by the revelation, or you may discover you are the last to know. Everyone else may know and have already forgiven. Check your motives and check with God.

Q: I'm a 40-year-old woman and I've never been married. I don't understand what I'm doing wrong. I'm starting to doubt that this will ever happen to me. Like most women I would like to have the experience of being married to someone I could spend the rest of my life with. I'm so afraid of being alone. What kind of advice can you give me? What type of prayer should I say for God to bless me with the right husband, and what should I believe? Signed: Why Not Me, Lord?

A: Dear Why Not Me, Lord?

Well, for one thing, you are putting the horse before the cart. The Bible instructs you to "seek ye first the kingdom of God and his righteousness, and all these things shall be added unto you" (Matthew 6:33 KJV). God is always with you. Therefore, you are never alone. Just rest in the Lord and wait patiently for Him to give you a mate. You are still very young; remember, 40 is the new 25! Often the unlimited opportunities of being single are overlooked because of the preoccupation with finding a mate.

The apostle Paul (who, by the way, was single) said in Philippians 4:11 that we should learn to be content in whatever state we find ourselves. No one can make you happy. That is too great a burden to put on another human being. You must learn to be happy and complete within yourself. Cultivate friendships with other singles; plan outings and trips. Widen your circle of interest by volunteering and doing missionary work. Being single, you have the freedom to make choices to enhance your life experience; that is, if you don't spend your time living in frustration always looking for "Mr. Right."

Unfortunately, when a person reaches their 30s (and in your case, their 40s) and is still unmarried, that person sees himself or herself as deficient. Many singles think, "If I could just be married, my life would be complete." Being married doesn't solve your problems. In fact, you carry problems with you into a marriage and they become compounded by the problems your spouse brings into the marriage as well. First Corinthians 7:27 tell us those who are married seek to be free and those who are free seek to be married. One counselor said, "Half of the people who come to me have problems because of their marriage, and the other half have problems because they are single!"

Now don't get me wrong, a good marriage is a blessing. However, developing a good relationship comes before a good marriage. You can't just jump out there and marry the first man who comes along. A good marriage is the result of two people who seek God's guidance. There are no formulas or prayers to get God to give you a husband.

If God has not given you the gift of singleness, then believe He desires for you to be married. I advise you to stop worrying, doubting, and being afraid and use your time and energy to prepare yourself to be a complete, well-rounded person. Then you will be ready to give and receive in marriage.

Q: I am 38 years old and am considered very successful by many, yet I am always alone. I do not want to hear that my position intimidates men because I never bring it up in a relationship. I know I have standards but why should I lessen them for a date that will never lead to anything? So I am now contemplating online dating. Is this considered outside the will of God? My friends tell me that "Who God has for me will show up in his timing" . . . but I feel the timing is off. Please help! Signed: Successful Without, Lonely Within

A: Dear Successful Without, Lonely Within,

Is online dating a sin? No. Is it advisable? No. Matchmaking websites are popping up daily, and online dating is an emerging trend among Christians. Proverbs 18:22 says, "Whoso findeth a wife findeth a good thing, and obtaineth favour of the Lord" (KJV). The purpose of Christian dating should be to find an appropriate mate, and as this Scripture indicates, the man should be doing the looking and finding. I know you may have heard success stories about online dating, but you have no idea who you will meet when you are online. Many impatient women have become victims by meeting people online. I urge caution. Consider the dangers inherent in meeting someone for a date neither your family nor friends know. Isaac's father Abraham sent one of his servants to find a mate for him. In those days, the father was responsible for making a good match for his children. It is still advisable to meet someone your family or friends can vouch for as a person of character and integrity. You should not lower your standards, and God's timing is never off. He is always on time. We sometimes struggle with waiting on the Lord and being "of good courage."

Q: I am so sick of my mother-in-law, who also is the pastor's wife. My husband and I have been married for almost three years and have not had a child. She continues to ask us why not. We both worked very hard through college and graduate schools. We just purchased our first home and are almost done paying off student loans. My mother-in-law acts as if I am embarrassing her by not being pregnant or active in the church. To top it off, she consistently reminds my husband, who is a CPA, his call is to be a pastor because her husband has built a mega church. Help me before she makes me want to move us or her out of the way! Signed: Can I Please Get a Witness?

A: Dear Can I Please Get a Witness?

Before you make a move you will regret, let me remind you that you do have a witness. According to Job 16:19, "Also now, behold, my witness is in heaven, and my record is on high" (KJV). The Lord knows your heart and the love you show to your husband and his mother. Regardless of what she says and does, the Lord still holds you accountable for your loving response. Remember your husband is her son, and it must be challenging for him to know the pain you both are experiencing. I appreciate your statement of honest emotion. You have a right to feel tired, sick, and frustrated; so does your mother-in-law.

Your mother-in-law has a vested interest in her son and her future legacy. As two wise women that love the same man, instead of resenting her, try to understand her.

Overbearing mothers-in-law are not new. They are usually well-meaning women who don't know how to let go. You sound as though you have endured a great deal. Do not throw away all your hard work. However, she cannot get you pregnant or live your life. The Lord gives life and allows us to be fruitful and multiply. It is up to God—not you, your husband, or your mother-in-law—to determine the appointed time God will allow you to conceive (if you are not interfering).

Concerning your husband's mother's belief that your husband has been called to the ministry: God calls into ministry, not parents. Your husband knows if such a call has been made on his life, and it is his responsibility to answer that call. Overall, it is your husband's responsibility to deal with his mother. He is now the head of his own household and should gently remind his mother of that fact. He should 1) thank his mother for her concern and advice; 2) remind her as the head of his household that he will seek God for the right decisions; and 3) explain that he and his wife are responsible to God for fulfilling their God-given roles in the marriage.

Praise God for your education and that you have been able to pay off your financial debts. Your mother-in-law can huff and puff, but she cannot blow your house down if it is built on the solid rock. However, you and your husband should keep the law of kindness in your mouth. As children, we also have a debt to our parents to honor them (Deuteronomy 5:16; Ephesians 6:2–3). The Deuteronomy parent-honoring command comes with the promise that it will go well with you. May you be pregnant with love and wisdom, and then deliver with grace.

Q: My boss is very belittling and condescending. Every day, I hate coming to work. However, I'm very good at my job and I receive a handsome salary. My office is located near my home, which stops the burden of dealing with the traffic others face every day. Other than dealing with him, my job is great. I'm very afraid one day I may blow up at him and lose my job because I have endured so much over the years. What can I do? I pray every morning prior to walking through those doors for peace! Signed: No More Cheeks to Turn!

A: Dear No More Cheeks to Turn!

Sounds like a wonderful job; you did not mention what you have endured, but any type of harassment on the job is unlawful. Sexual harassment is not the only kind of abuse we sometimes face in the workplace. When there is a problem on the job, ignoring it or just putting up with it never makes it go away or get better. Don't you dare blow up and lose that great job. After you have used up both your cheeks, just do something to put a stop to the harassment. Find out what your legal rights are, and then take the appropriate steps to resolve this issue and keep praying for peace. Opposition is a great opportunity to let your light shine brighter.

Begin to pray for your boss and others in the office who are being impacted by his inappropriate behavior. What is going on in his life or has happened to him that would lead to such public display of belittlement and condescending responses?

You have already used your cheeks. Now, use your knees— not to kick him, but to pray. Others are watching and probably waiting for the drama. Don't give them a show. God hears your cry. The Bible says in Romans 12:18, "If possible, so far as it depends on you, be at peace with all men." If peace is not possible in this situation and it has become unbearable, count the costs before you walk away from an otherwise wonderful job.

Remember, God can give you inner peace in the midst of outer turmoil.

Q: My sister is the other woman. She has been dating this guy for more than three years. His wife lives in another city with the children; he was transferred for a five-year assignment. My sister actually believes God sent this man to her because he is so unhappy and she makes him very happy. Her husband died suddenly from a massive heart attack, and she met this man a couple of months after his death. She said she had just finished praying, seeking an answer to her pain, and met him at the drugstore. I think my sister is depressed. This is not her character. She has always been a serious, no-nonsense, saved, respectful, and committed person. I have tried reasoning with her, I have tried sharing the Word with her (which she knows better than me) and I have tried shaming her, but nothing is working. Signed: I Need a Miracle

A: Dear I Need a Miracle,

Yes you do. Begin to fast and pray for divine intervention. Your sister is possibly delusional in addition to being depressed. She is substituting fantasy for reality. Even though she knows God hates adultery and fornication is a sin, she has convinced herself God has sanctioned this relationship.

She is running away from the grieving cycle. There is no way that she has dealt with all her emotions and resolved life issues regarding her loss in two months. She is using this man to avoid her pain, her emptiness, and to fill the void left by her husband's absence.

Your sister is in need of counseling and a strong reality check. Is there someone (other than you) that can do that for her? She is in shock. Thank God you know her and realize this is not typical of her character. Everyone needs someone in life who knew them when they were sane. Your sister is not in her right mind. Pray that the Lord reveals truth. If this relationship has been going on for more than three years, she will grieve twice when this is over. She will need those who truly love her to be close by and provide support.

The cycle of grief is filled with many emotions. Pray when she is delivered from this she does not fall into despair. God is able to keep her and restore her. He is a miracle-working God. As you lift up your sister, be mindful to pray for the family of this unfaithful man. Sin complicates things for all those involved.

Q: When I met my husband I thought he was so strong and protective; he picked the best restaurants and shows, and he always wanted me to have the best. My family and friends tried to tell me he was a control freak, but I just thought my friends were jealous and my family was still trying to tell me what to do. I was happy and blind until after the honeymoon, when he started vetoing every idea, thought, or change I had. Our life was wonderful as long as I said "Yes, honey" to everything he said. I thought it would get better, but we have been married a year now and it is worse than ever. I don't know what to do! I am so unhappy and ashamed of the way I dismissed my family and friends. I can't stand to hear them say "I told you so." I still love him and I believe he loves me. What can I do? Signed: Controlled

A: Dear Controlled,

When you feel smothered—with no choice, no voice, or no input into the relationship and no ability to make big or small decisions—you feel like a child. You are told what to do and how to do it. You may have limited access to financial resources, transportation, and other information. Controlling often masks as overprotection and sometimes feels abusive. It is difficult to have every move questioned and challenged. Many give in and acquiesce to the demands of their partner in order to minimize confusion and arguments. This type of relationship is stifling for the growth of the individuals and the marriage.

Your husband may have some misconceptions about each of your roles in the marriage. Genesis 2:18 defines the wife as a partner. She was made to help the man in accomplishing common goals. Furthermore, husbands and wives are to submit to one another (Ephesians 5:21; 1 Corinthians 7:3). If the woman was to stop thinking and acting on her own once she becomes a wife, then God would wrap her brains and emotions up in a nice little present for the husband upon the wedding day. Find an experienced counselor in your congregation you both trust and respect and seek counseling.

It is obvious your friends and family saw warning signs in this man and you refused to listen. Therefore, you may be outside of God's will by marrying. One of the first things you need to do is to ask God's forgiveness. Then, ask Him to restore you and give you the tools necessary to deal with your husband's overprotectiveness. Be honest with your husband. Ask him if you have done something to give him the impression you are incapable of making competent decisions.

Discuss your feelings about his controlling actions in a non-confrontational way. Negotiate.

Q: I am married with three children and a good husband whom I love dearly. We get along all right, but lately I noticed he does not want to be home much after work. He is spending more time with his friends at their homes. We have been fussing lately over life challenges and he is saying he would rather be elsewhere, where he can get peace and quiet, than at our house. What can I do to shape our home into the place where my spouse and children long to be? How do I turn my house into the haven that will keep my husband home and happy and give my children a protected location where they see the two of us getting along better? Signed: My Home Is Falling Apart

A: Dear My Home Is Falling Apart,

Please read Proverbs 31:10–31 and Ephesians 6:1–4; you will find them both very helpful. The Bible is a book filled with wise answers. Proverbs 17:1 tells us it is better to eat a dry morsel with quietness than to eat a feast where there is strife. It also says it is better to live alone in a tumbledown shack than share a mansion with a nagging spouse.

You and your husband need to take time to reassess your communication style. You must be able to voice your concerns with him without yelling and being accusatory. Being angry and contentious only increases the problem rather than fixing it. Therefore, you need to set aside a time when both of you are calm and willing to listen. "You must let no unwholesome word come out of your mouth, but only what is beneficial for the building up of the one in need, that it may give grace to those who hear" (Ephesians 4:29 NET).

You said your arguments are ongoing and affecting the household. Maybe you should step back from the problem and allow your husband to deal with it. God has placed him as the head of your household (Ephesians 5:22–25). Since you don't seem to be getting anywhere, you should let him know you are going to defer to him as the head and you will be praying for God's wisdom and guidance in each situation. Then do just that! Marriage is all about sacrifice. If you want a godly marriage, then you have to apply godly principles. This may just be the sacrifice God is looking for to show the light of Christ in you.

Your husband told you what he needs, so a good start would be to give the man what he asked for—some peace and quiet. Entice him back home with a well-prepared meal and some alone time. Maybe you can schedule a time to spend together after dinner, when you both are relaxed and not so stressed, to just have fun and enjoy each other's company. Proverbs 14:1 says, "A wise woman builds her home, but a foolish woman tears it down with her own hands" (NLT).

Q: My best friend is mostly a wonderful person. I say mostly because she has become a chronic complainer. She tells me all about her husband's shortcomings, as she calls them. We have known each other all our lives and I used to enjoy our fellowship, but now I dread it when she calls me. If she is not complaining about him, she is trying to fix me. How can I tell her I don't need to hear all about her husband's faults without offending her? I don't want to lose a lifelong friend. Signed: Please Help

A: Dear Please Help,

Complaining often takes the form of criticism. The Bible tells us it is better to live in a house with a continual drip than to live in a house with a nagging woman or man. Living with a critical or complaining person is draining. If your friend complains and criticizes her spouse until you (and him, most likely) are ready to scream, she needs to change and learn to view life differently. She needs to stop looking for things to complain about. She needs to look for the beautiful qualities in him that made her fall in love in the first place.

All complaints are not necessarily rooted in pessimism; some are actually legitimate concerns. But nagging and criticizing do not help, whether your friend complains to you or her spouse. Your friend is living in a pessimistic place, wrapped up in her situation; she may even derive comfort in her misery. She will ignore sound advice, and rebut your counsel with a litany of additional problems. She wants sympathy, not solutions.

Ask God to give you the grace to listen for a while, and then give you the wisdom to redirect the conversation away from the complaint to another subject. As Christians we want to glorify God and lead others to Him. In the midst of complaining, tell your friend you cannot fix the situation, but you are willing to pray with her about it. Then stop and do just that: pray! Remember you cannot change anyone else, so work on changing how you respond to her.

Q: Both my parents are over eighty and I am becoming their caregiver. It is so strange. I feel like my world has turned upside down. I just don't seem to have enough time to take care of everyone and everything. My husband expects me to keep the house clean, the meals ready, and the children disciplined as I did before I began caring for my parents. Can you give me some points on balancing my life and my parent's lives? Signed: I Need Balance

A: Dear I Need Balance,

Yes, you do. Not only do you need balance but you also need to have a conversation with your husband and others in your family who may have expectations of you, including siblings, children, your employer, and others to whom you have obligations. When our parents begin to age and need more of our time and attention, we do feel like our world is turned upside down. In order to get balance, you need to get understanding. You are only one person and you can only do so much. As a caregiver it is important for you to also care for yourself. If you don't take good care of you, then you will not be good to anyone else—your husband included.

Start by listing all of your duties and responsibilities; then identify who is available to help with each of these items. What will you need to let go as you assume the additional responsibilities in caring for your parents? It may be that your husband is not aware of everything required or the toll it takes on you daily. Caring for parents is more than just a list of to dos; it takes an emotional as well as physical toll. There may come a time when you have concerns about your parents living alone. Worries include using the stove, climbing stairs, healthy eating habits, exercise, and social activity.

It is always best to talk with your parents early before their living situation becomes an issue. Find out what they expect and how much you are willing to take on in light of your own situation. Pray for guidance and wisdom as you move forward. You want to honor your parents and your husband. Both of them are important primary relationships. However, if you do not have a conversation soon, you will end up bitter and resentful toward all of them as you give and give and give beyond what you have capacity to do.

If there are other family members, involve them in developing a plan for your parents' care. As the primary caregiver, you may need them to step in from time to time to give you some assistance. You may also need your husband to step in and give you some relief by assisting with the meals, cleaning, and caring for your children. This is a life-changing situation for you, and you need to be aware of the challenges ahead. Caring for elderly parents can be exhausting both mentally and physically, so make sure you set aside some personal time for yourself.

If there is no one else to give assistance, check out respite facilities where you can leave your parents for a few hours or even overnight. Some respite organizations can even assign a caregiver to your home for a few hours or several days a week. Remember, God knows how much you can bear even when others don't. We are oftentimes more resilient than we give ourselves credit for being. Give yourself permission to rest periodically, refuse certain tasks, and release the mixed emotions you will feel throughout this transition of life.

Q: We had several people over for the holiday. It was a mixture of family and friends, including a young married couple and their two children. The mother wore an extremely low-cut blouse that was offensive to me (and probably others as well). I never said anything to her. However, as I noticed her jiggle across the room on several occasions it brought to mind that she has worn inappropriate clothing to events in the past. How could I have handled this without it being offensive to her? Signed: Wanting to Be Appropriate with Those Who Are Not

A: Dear Wanting to Be Appropriate with Those Who Are Not,

Is this woman a family member, acquaintance, or friend? How often do you come in contact with her? If she is an acquaintance and her manner of dress is truly offensive to you, then you are under no obligation to invite her into your home again. However, you have no control over what she wears to other events. Unfortunately, the world is full of people who believe too tight, too short, too low, too tasteless clothing is fashionable. And while it certainly is a fashion faux pas to encourage people to believe spandex is for everyone, going to the other extreme to criticize anyone who dresses inappropriately doesn't work either.

If she is a family member and you do not feel comfortable talking to her, find out if there is someone who you think she will listen to and ask them to speak to her. However, maybe you could find an opportunity to take her aside and tactfully mention what she wears is unflattering or suggestive. She may not take kindly to the suggestion, but at least she will be aware what she may think looks good on her does not.

If this woman is a friend, then you are obligated to mention your concerns. The Bible says in Proverbs 27:6, "Faithful are the wounds of a friend; but the kisses of an enemy are deceitful"

(KJV). Perhaps she is not aware that she is being offensive in the way she dresses. Too many women buy into the hype that less is more, trashy is the new sexy, and if you got it, flaunt it. As a friend, you should be willing to take a chance on being honest with her. It may hurt her feelings temporarily, but it would be better than to also have others talking about her as well.

Now, in any of these three cases, if the woman is a Christian, she should be made aware it is her responsibility to be a role model for other Christian women (Titus 2:3–5). She can be stylish as well as modest. She can be fashionable and still godly. If she is open to the idea, have some fun going through each other's closets and clearing out the items that do not reflect Christian attire. You can also plan a day for shopping. This will give you an opportunity to see the types of clothing she likes and to gently guide her in a modest direction.

Q: My mother has been living with my husband and me for the past three years. She has been very ill. My four brothers have not been much help. They send money but always remind me they have families and just cannot do the daily activities. My husband and I have decided it is time to put her in hospice. The doctors can no longer do anything to sustain her and we can no longer afford 24/7 care. My brothers are angry with my husband and me about our decision. They don't seem to understand how much work is involved. Signed: She's Their Mom Too

A: Dear She's Their Mom Too,

It is a difficult situation when a loved one is in need of care. God has commanded us to love and honor our parents; take comfort that as you have lived in obedience to Him you will be blessed. There always seem to be some members of the family who will not do what we deem is their fair share. Try not to judge them, as they are dealing with their own set of circumstances. When you need help caring for the daily needs of your loved one, choosing hospice care can provide some relief for you and your family. They may also provide additional comfort and medical attention for your mother.

Don't feel guilty about making this decision. Many people seek hospice care when they have done all they can at home and the disease has a terminal prognosis. Hospice care can also offer you support and help you deal with the emotional stress of the changes taking place in your life and in your mother's life.

God will help you in this trying time. Turn to Him in faith and hear the encouraging words of Isaiah 40:28–31: "Have you not known? Have you not heard? The Lord is the everlasting God, the Creator of the ends of the earth. He does not faint or grow weary; his understanding is unsearchable. He gives power to the faint, and to him who has no might he increases strength. Even youths shall faint and be weary, and young men shall fall exhausted; but they who wait for the Lord shall renew their strength; they shall mount up with wings like eagles; they shall run and not be weary; they shall walk and not faint" (ESV).

As God comforts you, seek to show compassion for your brothers. When your mother passes, you and your brothers will still be here to reconcile your differences. The Bible charges you in Romans 12:18, "If it is possible, as much as lieth in you, live peaceably with all men" (KJV). Your brothers may not understand the decisions you and your husband are making. Invite them to be a part of what is being done. Maybe they will have some ideas or offer assistance or even emotional support. As you have indicated, she is their mom too.

Q: My mom and dad have been divorced since I was 16 years old. They still fight like cats and dogs and are always contacting each other for one reason or another. Then they call me to take sides. The issues they argue about are so trivial. Neither of them has remarried, although both of them dated other people years ago. Whenever there is a family event they promise to come at different times but somehow show up together and make a scene. I am so tired of being in the middle. When I talk with them it is usually about what the other one is doing now or has recently said. I no longer want to be the referee. Signed: Dropping the Flags in Florida

A: Dear Dropping the Flags in Florida,

Your parents have established a very dysfunctional relationship that is somehow working for them. They may never change and there is nothing you can do to change them; however, you can remove yourself from the position of referee. You are an adult now and they are hanging on to you as the glue that causes them to interact with each other. They will always be your parents, but they no longer make decisions for you, nor should you make decisions for them. Your parents may have numerous reasons for disagreeing but you do not have to be in the middle. Set some boundaries in your life and refuse to take sides. Graciously consider setting a timer and letting your parents know there is a limit on how much time you will spend discussing the other person and absolutely refuse to pass on any information.

If your parents don't comply, you can also consider limiting your time altogether until such time as they change their behavior. It may be hard to believe but there are people who actually like to fuss and fight. They don't try to avoid each other; they have instead made bickering a way of life. The Bible talks a lot in Proverbs about those who are cantankerous, spiteful, rabble rousers, and even foolish. People who like drama need prayer. Please spend some time in prayer before you drop the flags or approach your parents. Dealing with parents who raised you can be sensitive, especially if they feel their behavior is being challenged. Ask God to give you wisdom so you can honor your parents even as you draw the line.

Q: My little sister, who is 14, is the primary caregiver for my mom's 8-year-old son by her third husband. I'm not passing judgment but there are four of us—all with different dads. William has cerebral palsy. Jen has been taking care of him since he was born, while my mom works. She has missed most of her childhood. I'm concerned that she is also going to miss out on all the wonderful things about being a teenager. I want to ask her to come live with me. My mom's new husband makes enough money for her to just stay home and raise her son. I believe she works so that she doesn't have to deal with William. Am I wrong for wanting to rescue Jen? Signed: Sister to the Rescue

A: Dear Sister to the Rescue,

I understand your concern for your sister. But remember you are on the outside looking in. Don't jump to conclusions without all the facts. You don't know what the financial arrangements are in their household. Your mother may have to work.

All siblings at some point provide care for one another. How much time is spent varies from house to house depending on the situation. You say you are not judging but it does sound as though you take issue with your mother's choices. Some of the things you are concerned about were God's choices. He is aware of your sister's situation. God placed her in this family with these circumstances. He knows. Maybe God is doing a mighty work in her and this experience will be needed to help prepare her for a great destiny. Her future ministry calling may be connected to what she is presently doing.

Have you tried talking over your concerns with your mother? Maybe you and your mother together can provide some relief for your little sister. Why don't you try helping your sister by relieving her as you take on some of her childcare duties, thus allowing her some free time to play? I want to caution you that taking on the full-time care of a teenager is a big undertaking for anyone at any age. Think long and seriously before you seek to make any changes to other people's lives. Your sister may be very happy with being able to provide care for her brother and may not feel that she is missing out on as much as you think.

Q: I have a girlfriend that's very gullible when it comes to men. As a consequence, she makes bad decisions, and then asks why this has happened to her. I've shared with her that the answers she seeks concerning relationships with men are in the Bible, but she still continues to believe she has the right answers to everything without noticing she doesn't. I'm now to the point that just speaking with her about her problems has frustrated me and I want to discontinue our friendship all together. I'm also to the point that I'm becoming rude! How can I minister to her and not display my total disgust with her lack of receiving? Signed: Birds of a Feather Don't Flock Together!

A: Dear Birds of a Feather Don't Flock Together!

A friend knows and exercises the proper approach in various situations. There is a time to warn and admonish, as well as a time to encourage. At all times when we confront sin in the lives of others, we should speak the truth in love in a spirit of gentleness and meekness. Consider that Paul admonished us to be mindful that we all were there once. You did not always make the right decisions or heed godly counsel. We learn God is longsuffering with us and has loved us to repentance. As we grow and change, God gives us opportunities to help others achieve the same success by applying the Word of God, modeling appropriate behavior, and sharing our testimony. As a Christian, you may want to demonstrate the same grace and mercy to your friend God extended to you. If you want to see your friend soar in her relationship with God and with others, then don't abandon her—teach her to fly.

LET US PRAY

Father, in the name of the Lord Jesus Christ, I thank you that you are a relational God. You understand how I sometimes struggle with my relationships. Help me to honor and respect everyone, especially my own mother and father. Help me to see their actions as love with the intent to help, not as intrusions into my lives. I thank you, Father, for being a friend that stays closer to me than a brother. I want to be like you and befriend others without judging them. Help me to be that way with my friends. Help me not to be a people-pleaser. I want my relationships to be pleasing to you. Lord, please work in my heart so that I will honor and respect those under my authority in the same way I do those in authority over me. I want to be a person of integrity in my dealings with others. I pray that all of my relationships will help me to bring glory to the name of Christ. Lord, help me to be loving, giving, and forgiving.

Scripture Truth to Help You LIVE RIGHT NOW

Category: RELATIONSHIPS

Then the man said, "This at last is bone of my bones and flesh of my flesh; she shall be called Woman, because she was taken out of Man." Therefore a man shall leave his father and his mother and hold fast to his wife, and they shall become one flesh. And the man and his wife were both naked and were not ashamed.

Genesis 2:23–25 (ESV)

Honor your father and your mother, that your days may be long in the land that the LORD your God is giving you.

Exodus 20:12 (ESV)

Therefore, if anyone is in Christ, he is a new creation. The old has passed away; behold, the new has come. All this is from God, who through Christ reconciled us to himself and gave us the ministry of reconciliation.

2 Corinthians 5:17–18 (ESV)

[Walk] with all humility and gentleness, with patience, showing tolerance for one another in love, being diligent to preserve the unity of the Spirit in the bond of peace.

Ephesians 4:2–3

Love is patient, love is kind, and is not jealous; love does not brag and is not arrogant, does not act unbecomingly; it does not seek its own, is not provoked, does not take into account a wrong suffered, does not rejoice in unrighteousness, but rejoices with the truth; bears all things, believes all things, hopes all things, endures all things. Love never fails; but if there are gifts of prophecy, they will be done away; if there are tongues, they will cease; if there is knowledge, it will be done away.

1 Corinthians 13:4–8

And let us consider how to stimulate one another to love and good deeds, not forsaking our own assembling together, as is the habit of some, but encouraging one another; and all the more, as you see the day drawing near.

Hebrews 10:24–25

He who walks with wise men will be wise, But the companion of fools will suffer harm.

Proverbs 13:20

Above all, keep loving one another earnestly, since love covers a multitude of sins.

1 Peter 4:8 (ESV)

Let love be genuine. Abhor what is evil; hold fast to what is good. Love one another with brotherly affection. Outdo one another in showing honor.

Romans 12:9–10 (ESV)

Do not rebuke an older man but encourage him as you would a father, younger men as brothers, older women as mothers, younger women as sisters, in all purity.

1 Timothy 5:1–7 (ESV)

Do not be deceived: "Bad company ruins good morals."

1 Corinthians 15:33 (ESV)

Do not be unequally yoked with unbelievers. For what partnership has righteousness with lawlessness? Or what fellowship has light with darkness?

2 Corinthians 6:14 (ESV)

Live the Word. Live Right Now Application

Select five verses about relationships from the previous pages and complete these exercises.

Verse # 1 _____

How would you summarize this verse of Scripture?

_____

_____

_____

_____

What does the Bible verse mean to you? _____

_____

_____

_____

Does this verse give you instructions for hope, help, or healing?

_____

As you read this Scripture verse, do you feel the need to repent, reflect, or rejoice? _____

What do you need to do differently to live right now?

_____

_____

Name at least one person to whom you can be accountable and share your decision to live right now.

_____

Name at least one person you can encourage by sharing this Scripture.

_____

Verse # 2 _____

How would you summarize this verse of Scripture?

_____

_____

_____

_____

What does the Bible verse mean to you? _____

_____

_____

_____

Does this verse give you instructions for hope, help, or healing?

_____

As you read this Scripture verse, do you feel the need to repent, reflect, or rejoice? _____

What do you need to do differently to live right now?

_____

_____

Name at least one person to whom you can be accountable and share your decision to live right now.

_____

Name at least one person you can encourage by sharing this Scripture. _____

_____

Verse # 3 _____

How would you summarize this verse of Scripture?

_____

_____

_____

_____

What does the Bible verse mean to you? _____

_____

_____

Does this verse give you instructions for hope, help, or healing?

_____

As you read this Scripture verse, do you feel the need to repent, reflect, or rejoice? _____

What do you need to do differently to live right now?

_____

_____

_____

Name at least one person to whom you can be accountable and share your decision to live right now.

_____

Name at least one person you can encourage by sharing this Scripture.

_____

Verse # 4 _____

How would you summarize this verse of Scripture?

_____

_____

_____

_____

What does the Bible verse mean to you? _____

_____

_____

_____

_____

Does this verse give you instructions for hope, help, or healing?

_____

As you read this Scripture verse, do you feel the need to repent, reflect, or rejoice? _____

What do you need to do differently to live right now?

_____

_____

Name at least one person to whom you can be accountable and share your decision to live right now.

_____

Name at least one person you can encourage by sharing this Scripture. _____

Verse # 5 _____

How would you summarize this verse of Scripture?

_____

_____

_____

What does the Bible verse mean to you?

_____

_____

_____

Does this verse give you instructions for hope, help, or healing?

_____

As you read this Scripture verse, do you feel the need to repent, reflect, or rejoice? _____

What do you need to do differently to live right now?

_____

_____

_____

Name at least one person to whom you can be accountable and share your decision to live right now.

_____

Name at least one person you can encourage by sharing this Scripture.

_____

CHAPTER 2

CHURCH AND RELIGION

You can be committed to church and not committed to Christ; but you cannot be committed to Christ and not committed to church.

Joel Osteen

Then Peter and the other apostles answered and said, We ought to obey God rather than men.

Acts 5:29 (KJV)

The questions and or insinuations that abound in our society today are: "Do we really need the church or religion?" "Is the church effective today?" and "Is the church accomplishing the goals of the Bible?" In the interest of understanding the confusion, we must separate church and religion. Any object, practice, cause, activity, or a set of strongly held beliefs, values, and attitudes that anyone is completely devoted to or obsessed by can be called their religion, because they serve whatever it is dutifully, consistently, unfailingly, devotedly, and loyally. Religion is also considered a system or set of rules and guidelines followed with faith and conviction.

The church is a group of people acting as a single entity, able to come into agreement around God's Word and be of one accord, as the church serves Him dutifully, consistently, devotedly, and loyally. The purpose of the church is threefold: 1) to evangelize non-believers, 2) to edify and equip those who believe, and 3) to exalt the One in whom we believe, Jesus Christ our Lord.

We are the church, the body of Christ, and we should operate as one in corporate solidarity. Each individual serves as a part of the group because of their connection with the head of the group. The people in a group give support to each other because they have the same opinions, goals, and/or leader.

The Old Testament presents the principles and standards of corporate solidarity. In biblical times, people lived with a oneness mind-set. Acts 2:44 indicates all the believers had all things in common. In another time, the motto might have been, "One for all and all for one!"

Today's motto is just the opposite: "Look out for 'numero uno' (number one)," or another version: "The only thing that matters is me, myself, and I." That mind-set makes the idea of corporate solidarity difficult for us to accept and understand. This concept can appear to be unjust or unfair to the worldly mind. This idea also leads some people to believe they don't need others in their lives. The thought of gathering one or two times weekly for worship, fellowship, accountability, or any spiritual reason is perceived as needy and far too dependent. The self-sacrificial orientation strikes the world as strange.

"Are you religious?" "Do you go to church?" These are the questions that immediately come to mind when assessing one's spirituality. But these are the wrong questions for those who profess Christ. The questions that get to the heart of the matter look more like this: "Do your actions and character reflect Jesus Christ?" "Do you have a relationship with God and are you living for Him?" The Bible tells us in James 1:27, "Religion that is pure and undefiled before God the Father, is this; to visit orphans and widows in their affliction, and to keep oneself unstained or unspotted from the world" (ESV).

The church represents the body of Christ. Every person who believes has the opportunity to share in Christ's forgiveness, the indwelling of the Holy Spirit, and the confidence of His presence to help in times of need. For those of us who profess Christ, it is when we are applying the Word of God in our lives and making clear choices for the kingdom that those around realize that we are neither mindless nor foolish, but intentional.

There are many myths surrounding the church and religion. Those who do not attend church see it as just a building for gathering. Those who are in the church—that is, the body of Christ—recognize the church is a sacred space, but also that individuals are really the building—the temple of God. Christians are faith believers, which means we believe even when there is no evidence of what we are hoping to see come to pass. Faith believers know without a doubt that it is impossible to live life without faith. Our faith represents a substance built on hope, from an evidence of many things we as a people could not even begin to fathom as reality, except as a result of our experience with God. Therefore, to live, walk, and move on the principles of faith means exhibiting the courage to turn away from man's way of doing things, and turn to God's ways even when we are unsure of the outcome. Faith must begin in the mind and heart of the individual believer.

People today, like generations before them, are looking for something. They are longing to develop relationships and discover meaning in life. They may not be aware that until they achieve intimacy with Christ, no other relationship matters or satisfies. Even as they look for meaning in life, they bypass the good news of the gospel of Jesus Christ. People are willing to try sex, drugs, alternative lifestyles, eastern religions, the occult, and all the things they mistakenly believe will afford them the peace they seek. Although temporary relief may be achieved, it is never enough to truly satisfy the longing of the soul. What man needs is an authentic connection with Christ that brings love, joy, and true peace—a peace that really does pass all human understanding.

> **People today, like generations before them, are looking for something. They are longing to develop relationships and discover meaning in life.**

The church should be known by its love for other people, without regard to their ethnicity, creed, social status, educational background, financial position, or past. Love is the unifying factor that draws and keeps us together as the body of Christ. Loving others as Christ loved us, unconditionally and sacrificially, is always relevant and never goes out of style. When we as believers live and love this way, we help the world overcome some of the many reasons they give for not accepting Christ or going to church.

You may have heard some of the reasons people do not accept Christ: the services are boring, churches are too strict, life is fine just the way it is, I like to (golf/rest/work/exercise) on Sunday, church people are hypocrites . . . the list of excuses is endless. Rather than pointing at and blaming the unbeliever, the church needs to look at itself. When our lifestyles do not reflect the importance of church, religion, and most of all Christ in our lives, we send a confusing message even as we tell the world "I am a Christian." We cannot afford to vacillate between the ways of the world and the Word of God.

> **When our lifestyles do not reflect the importance of church, religion, and most of all Christ in our lives, we send a confusing message even as we tell the world "I am a Christian."**

The same power God uses to save us and transform us can also help empower us to live more effectively as a community of faith believers. A close personal relationship with Jesus Christ helps us feel alive and dynamic. When we gain a deeper understanding of the Word of God and apply His principles in our daily lives, we can share the truth of God's Word and the accountability found at church as we deal with life problems, concerns, learning experiences, and the struggle to live right in a world doing wrong.

The Word of God is rich with instructions for people who believe in Jesus Christ. The apostle Paul was so committed to see the people grow in the churches he established that he wrote often about how they should live. What he had to say to the church at Ephesus, I say to all of you reading this book:

So I tell you this, and insist on it in the Lord, that you must no longer live as the Gentiles do, in the futility of their thinking. They are darkened in their understanding and separated from the life of God because of the ignorance that is in them due to the hardening of their hearts. Having lost all sensitivity, they have given themselves over to sensuality so as to indulge in every kind of impurity, and they are full of greed. That, however, is not the way of life you learned when you heard about Christ and were taught in him in accordance with the truth that is in Jesus. You were taught, with regard to your former way of life, to put off your old self, which is being corrupted by its deceitful desires; to be made new in the attitude of your minds; and to put on the new self, created to be like God in true righteousness and holiness. (Ephesians 4:17–24 NIV)

When you are ready to live right now, you must ignore the insinuations of society and adhere to the words of sound doctrine and good teaching about living the life of a Christian.

Do a quick assessment of these essential godly qualities and then read on:

- Faith
- Leadership
- Making Godly Choices
- Service
- Forgiveness

Q: I want to know how to keep my spiritual light lit. I attend church on a regular basis and read my Bible daily, yet some days are harder than others. I'm trying to maintain my faith. Is there a prayer that I can say to help me during the day? Signed: Someone Save My Soul

A: Dear Someone Save My Soul,

When you believe in your heart and confess with your mouth that Jesus Christ is Lord, you become a Christian. Jesus will begin to rule and reign in your life as you submit to the direction of the Holy Spirit. Don't struggle. When you trust and obey God, your spiritual light will burn brighter and brighter every day. As we keep our spiritual light lit, we learn the secrets of intimacy (unity, oneness, communion, fellowship). Like any other relationship, becoming a Christian on fire for the Lord is a lifestyle and it takes time.

When you wake up in the morning and before your feet hit the floor, thank God for waking you up and allowing you to experience another day—a day to be God's witness in the earth, telling others of His goodness. There may be some great Christian TV programs you can watch. You may want to identify two or three Scriptures with significant meaning for you and recite them to yourself throughout the course of every day. When you are going through a trial or temptation, remind yourself God's grace is sufficient for you.

You sound like a Christian woman who is actively working to mature in the faith. Reading your Bible and attending church regularly will help you stay strong and maintain your faith, because faith comes by hearing and hearing by the Word of God.

As a Christian woman, your soul is saved, but you are not exempt from the trials and hardships of life. There are times when we feel overwhelmed by the circumstances of life. Just remember, God asked us to cast all our cares upon Him because He cares for us. On your hard days, lean on Jesus and trust Him to help you. He has promised you the victory when you depend on Him. When you lean on the Lord, you let your light shine before the world and God receives all the glory.

Pray the Word of God; find those Scriptures that promise what you need. For example, "Father, I thank you that I can do all things because you strengthen me. Thank you that you have not given me a spirit of fear, but of love and of power and of a sound mind." If you would like a specific prayer, consider any of the prayers of the Apostle Paul:

- Romans 15:5–6, 13
- Ephesians 1:16–19
- Ephesians 3:16–19
- Philippians 1:9–11
- Colossians 1:9–12
- Hebrews 13:20–21

May you know the love of God and be strengthened in your inner being.

Q: My pastor is engaged to a woman who is not in church. She does not confess to be saved and is known as a loose woman and party girl. No, I am not interested in my pastor in any kind of way other than as a man of God. I just do not understand what message he is giving our congregation. He preaches righteousness and sanctification. He encourages us as single females to not try to minister to an unsaved man while dating him, yet here he stands in the pulpit and announces his engagement to a woman we never see in church, Bible study, or any other place of worship. Please, please explain this to me! Signed: What Exactly Does Unequally Yoked Mean?

A: Dear What Exactly Does Unequally Yoked Mean?

I should know; I wrote the book: *Can Two Walk Together? Spiritual Encouragement for Unequally Yoked Marriages.* The Bible defines "unequally yoked" three ways: only one spouse is saved (has a relationship with Christ), the spouses are of different religions, or one spouse is growing spiritually (and in other areas) and the other is not. The apostle Paul admonishes us in 2 Corinthians 6:14 to "be ye not unequally yoked together with unbelievers" (KJV). This applies to the members and the leaders of any church. It is important for us to walk circumspectly at all times because people are watching. The behavior of all Christians can be in question when one acts carnally.

The term loose, which you use to describe the woman your pastor is considering, is a nondescript word. It can mean everything and nothing. On what are you basing this evaluation? Does she not meet God's standards, or is it your standards where she falls short? How do you know whether or not she is saved? The Lord sees the heart. Have you witnessed her behavior or have you been entertaining gossip and slander? Just because you have not seen her at your church does not mean she does not go or that she does not love the Lord. This is a great opportunity for prayer as well as ministry. The Lord may desire to use you to restore her reputation. Consider keeping company with her and helping her learn the ways of God.

The church is your business and the pastor is blessed to have you as such a caring member. If you trust your pastor to be godly man who loves the Lord and teaches the Word of God, then trust him to know what he is doing. If you have the ear and heart of your pastor, pray and go to him. Let your pastor know people are talking about him and the woman he intends to marry. You want him to be aware before it gets out of hand. Let him know people in the congregation think he has been overtaken in a fault. Explain to your pastor you are not sure what the truth is, but you know him to be a man of God and want to give him an opportunity to address the matter.

In the meantime, pray and do not engage in conversations with others regarding the matter. Do not stand quietly by while others criticize. Do not receive an accusation against your pastor. God's Word refers to all of us as loose women, adulterers, backsliders, and lovers of the world and not God. Yet He loves us and continues to woo us. Read the book of Hosea to get a greater understanding of how God might work in these situations. Leave the judging to God.

Q: I am so torn. I am in love and my boyfriend keeps pressing me to have sex with him. I really want to please him, but I am saved and I know it would be a sin. I am not ready to give myself to anyone yet. I have always dreamed of saving myself for my husband. After our last date, we had a big fight and I cried myself to sleep. I keep wondering if he is right and I am wrong. After all, I am 23 and may still be single for a while yet. He said I was wasting my best sexual years. Why should I hide my body and not enjoy myself while I am at the peak of my beauty? Please help me. I am trying to hold on to my virginity. Signed: Barely Holding On

A: Dear Barely Holding On,

You stated you are "saved," which means God has set you apart from the things of the world. While God understands we make mistakes, you should not compromise your beliefs for the sole purpose of satisfying your boyfriend. You would not only be making a mistake but a clear choice to ignore God's Word on sex before marriage. Planning to stay a virgin until marriage is not wrong or a waste of time. It is the right thing to do. In life, there are no guarantees. Who is to say that your boyfriend will remain in your life after you have sex with him?

If your boyfriend really cares for you, he will respect your feelings and not attempt to persuade you to do otherwise for his pleasure. He should not attempt to convince you to go against God's Word and what you believe is right. You will also encounter the effects of going against biblical teachings regarding premarital sex. A lot of times, men are challenged when a woman does not give in to them sexually and will continue to try to pressure them until they give in. After they give in, the excitement the male experienced during the hunt is gone. He has chased you down like a deer; then after he has made the kill or conquest he is off on the next hunt. Or if you allow your boyfriend to engage in sex with you, what reason would he have to stop? Before you know it, it could last for weeks, months, even years with no commitment made to you. Hold fast to your belief! Stay true to yourself and your God. Continue to save yourself for your husband. You will be happy you did.

Q: My life has been average. Nothing really bad has happened to me but nothing really good either. I'm 28 years old, single with a boyfriend. Among my friends none of us have children outside of marriage. My parents are alive and healthy. I have no complaints. I like my job and make decent money. So, why am I writing you? I feel like a robot going through the motions. I pray but I'm not sure God hears me and I'm not sure what path my life is on. It feels like I am not going anywhere, just living day after day more of the same old thing. Signed: Bored

A: Dear Bored,

Have you received Jesus as your Lord and Savior? If you have a personal relationship with Jesus Christ, you can be sure God always hears you when you pray. Ask God to show you His purpose for your life, and to direct your path. God has exciting plans for you! He has wonderful works designed just for you to do. Turn to God in faith and start a new life full of adventure; you will never be bored again.

What you described is not an average life. Yours is a life filled with God's grace! Everything that happened in your life has been good. Apparently your parents loved you and raised you with good moral qualities. You have friends and a boyfriend. You must have received an education to have a job you like with good pay. Your parents are alive and healthy. I have an important question for you. Where were you when all of these wonderful things were happening in your life? Wake up. You are no robot. You are an expression of God's love, created in His image. You are fearfully and wonderfully made—a unique masterpiece, one of a kind.

Q: Each time I hear of a preacher in trouble because of misuse of funds or sexual misconduct, the first thing members say is, "Touch not God's anointed." Well, aren't all who believe His anointed? Why do people believe preachers are special? Signed: Are There Big I's and Little Me's?

A: Dear Are There Big I's and Little Me's?

The short answer is no. We are all servants of the Most High God! So why do people believe preachers are special? It's because they are! (We are all special to God!) First Timothy 5:17 says, "Let the elders that rule well be counted worthy of double honour, especially they who labour in the word and doctrine" (KJV). Leaders in the church should be respected and given honor if they are truly teaching the principles and precepts of God, and are walking worthy of the vocation unto which they were called.

First Timothy 5:19–21 says that if there are at least two witnesses accusing an elder and if the elder has sinned, he is to be rebuked. It does not say we are to sit back and let God correct him if he's done wrong! "Brethren, if a man be overtaken in a fault, ye which are spiritual, restore such an one in the spirit of meekness; considering thyself, lest thou also be tempted" (Galatians 6:1 KJV). Preachers are human beings possessing the same frailties we have, so you should keep them in prayer; especially if they have fallen and are now asking for forgiveness of sin. If there is humility and repentance, we should work to restore the repentant one to usefulness in the body of Christ.

All Christians who truly follow Christ and have been sealed with the Holy Spirit—not just ministers—are the anointed of God. Second Corinthians 1:20–22 says, "For no matter how many promises God has made, they are 'Yes' in Christ. And so through him the 'Amen' is spoken by us to the glory of God. Now it is God who makes both us and you stand firm in Christ. He anointed us, set his seal of ownership on us, and put his Spirit in our hearts as a deposit, guaranteeing what is to come" (NIV). We are all set aside for a purpose and function in the body of Christ. Whatever God called you to do, you are held accountable to that area of ministry. As Christians, we should all walk worthily.

Q: I feel as if I am no longer of any worth in the kingdom of God! I had so much hope and joy when my husband was called to start a church almost twenty years ago. We were excited about being used by God and we were happy and busy right from the start. It's hard to say when things started to change. I just know we are overwhelmed; we are both extremely tired. Our time together has turned into a mutual complaining session. We have started avoiding each other and our kids act as if they hate us and the church. To make matters worse, the church I love seems to take our service for granted. I feel like calling it quits. I don't want to abandon my husband in the work and I'm sure I would be even unhappier if I quit but I just have to get away and try to sort things out before I lose it. What can I do? I still love God and my family. Signed: I Can't Quit

A: Dear I Can't Quit,

It is an occupational hazard for those in ministry to experience compassion fatigue—to become disillusioned, disappointed, disgruntled, discouraged, and even fall into despair. The people God called us to serve often wound us. When clergy leaders are overworked, overwhelmed, and overextended, they need to get a break or get away. The problem becomes paramount when you wait too long to do self-care. When this happens, we tend to just run away or get away to the wrong things. If things are hard on you, imagine what it must be like for him. The things I share with you can also be a blessing to your husband.

The Bible admonishes us in Galatians 6:9 as well as 2 Thessalonians 3:13 to "grow not weary in well doing" (doing good, doing right, doing it God's way), but it also tells us from the words of Jesus in Matthew 11:28, "Come unto me all you who labor [are burdened] and are heavy laden, and I will give you rest" (NKJV). In my experience, clergy from one denomination to the next struggle with the balance between working 24/7 and finding time to slip away from the crowd to spend time with God so that they can rest and be replenished. Jesus is the perfect example for holy, stress-free living. Read the Scriptures below and follow Jesus' example.

- Matthew 14:13–23
- Mark 1:32–37
- Mark 6:30–32

Here are five things to remember:

1. Follow Jesus' model of ministry. He served. He rested. He ministered. He rested. He came apart from the crowds to pray and to replenish. This is God's way.

2. Remember to practice what you preach. Live the Word. The Bible has answers. Encourage yourself in the Word. Speak life to your situation. Practice love and forgiveness constantly.

3. Remember it was God who called you. It was not by your choosing. It was not by chance or happenstance. Ministry is much more than a profession or a vocation it is a lifestyle.

4. Remember your mission. You've been called to be the "under-shepherd" of the "Great Shepherd" representing God to sheep who, yes, sometimes bite the hands that feed them. You are God's messenger. He is the message. Allow His love to flow through you and keep His Word on your lips. Your mission field is the world. Your mandate is to "preach the gospel" empowered by the Spirit of the Lord.

5. Remember you are not alone. Sometimes the weight of the ministry seems so heavy you don't know how much longer you can endure. But remember, with the weight, there is His glory if you bear it and don't run away by forsaking your calling. God has not abandoned you. You are not alone. Others have been where you are and have overcome. You are not alone. The angels of the Lord are encamped round about you. God has assigned someone somewhere to serve as your armor

bearer to help to carry the weight. You are not alone. The Holy Spirit is also on assignment to comfort you. You are not alone. God sent me to assist with godly counsel.

Although you are tired, I'm glad you realize you cannot quit. God called you to service and He is also calling you to come rest in Him. Shut off as many things as you can (cell phones, computers, television, etc.) and shut out as many people as you can, so you can have some alone time with God. Allow the Lord to minister to you so you can continue your ministry to others.

Q: I'm a 30-year-old woman who has been married for three years. How can I get my husband interested in church? He believes in God and attended church as a child, but as an adult he doesn't feel the need to attend anymore. His point of view is that all pastors are kickoff pimps and game runners and that is why he believes church members consist of 80 percent women. Please show me how to change his mind. Signed: For Better or Worse

A: Dear For Better or Worse,

Changing your husband is not your responsibility. Living a righteous life as a child of God and praying for him is the thing for you to do. His mind will not be changed until God changes his heart. Unfortunately some pastors and churches use the Word of God to their own advantage. It is not for us to judge, God will deal with them. Revelation tells us in the last days there will be many false prophets (pimps and game runners). God will separate the wheat from the chaff.

Most men don't want to be caught up in hypocrisy or mess, nor do they have time for church politics. In the words of my husband, "leave him alone and he will come home wagging his tail behind him." As the Lord opens his eyes and his ears, his desire for godly things will change. Pray for him and trust God to bring him into the ark of safety. Love him into the faith; don't condemn him. There are several great books that may help you. Don't disagree with your husband when he speaks the truth. Acknowledging and validating the truth he shares with you will position him to acknowledge the truth you share with him.

This is one of the key areas addressed in my book, *Can Two Walk Together?* I could not understand why my husband wanted nothing to do with God or the church. However, when I was unequally yoked, God revealed to me that the light of my life magnified the darkness in my husband's life. All of my well-meant intentions to help him grow up in the faith were misinterpreted as pious and holier than thou. David Burrow has this to say in his book, *Why Men Hate Going to Church*:

> Let me be blunt: today's church has developed a culture that is driving men away. Almost every man in America has tried church, but two-thirds find it unworthy of a couple of hours once a week. A wise Texan once told me, "Men don't go to church 'cuz they've been." When men need spiritual sustenance, they go to the wilderness, the workplace, the garage, or the corner bar. Church is one of the last places men look for God.

It is God's will for all men to live saved and grow into the fullness of Him. Pray for your husband that God's will be done in his life. Be consistent in your endeavors to walk your talk. Live before your husband the life you profess and your actions will invite him to grow in God.

Q: I'm a 25-year-old young woman and very new to the Word of God! Is it a sin to listen to worldly music? I enjoy my Lyfe Jennings, Kem, and other R&B singers. Their music has meaning without calling women out of their names, gang banging, and dope selling. Is it wrong to listen to worldly music with positive meaning? Signed: Music for the Soul

A: Dear Music for the Soul,

Praise God that as a new Christian you are seeking godly advice on how to live your life! There is a continual debate in Christendom regarding music as to whether Christian artists should sing secular songs—usually defined by the fact that the artists did not say one of the key words for Christianity (God, Jesus, and Holy Spirit)—or if their music should be played on non-Christian stations. Some say it is not wrong to listen to any secular music as long as you interpret it right; others would advise you to take all of your CDs and albums and burn them because the content is unholy. I say, if it causes you to sin, stop listening to it. Do the lyrics line up with Scripture? Fine. Do they cause you to violate and disobey the authorities in your life (parents, pastors, or spouse)? Do they cause other people in your life to stumble into sin? Are they filled with swearing or false messages about life? Not fine.

Many parents argue they need to listen to even raunchy secular music because of their children; they want to know what they are being exposed to when they are with their peers. That is a valid point, but even that should be limited, merely for information and understanding. The Word of God tells us in Philippians 4:8: "Finally, brothers and sisters, whatever is true, whatever is noble, whatever is right, whatever is pure, whatever is lovely, whatever is admirable—if anything is excellent or praiseworthy—think about [or listen to] such things" (NIV).

Music often communicates a message, tells a story, or brings to your remembrance a situation or experience. The questions for any Christian to ask about music are: Where does the music take you? What is it speaking to you? And what is it inspiring in you—good or evil? Will the music bring edification to you or others? Will the music glorify God or draw people to Him?

I recall being at a symphony and just moved to tears at the magnificence of the musical composition. Truly the instrumental arrangement I heard had to be God-inspired. As often as you can, live as the fulfillment of Scripture. "Speaking to yourselves in psalms and hymns and spiritual songs, singing and making melody in your heart to the Lord" (Ephesians 5:19 KJV). "Let the word of Christ dwell in you richly in all wisdom; teaching and admonishing one another in psalms and hymns and spiritual songs, singing with grace in your hearts to the Lord" (Colossians 3:16 KJV).

Q: I often hear from Christians who have become disillusioned with the concept of going to church, whether it is a bad experience or church members making them feel uncomfortable, or just the fact that they woke up too late to get their families together to attend. In most cases they've given up entirely on the practice of attending a local church and justify their decision by sitting in front of their televisions. I always say one of the following statements to these people, "When you need food or clothing, you go to the grocery or department store!" "When your car is in need of repair, you take it to a mechanic!" or "When you get a new job, you're required to take a training class from someone with more experience!"

Other than explaining that attending church allows you a time to worship God in song and prayer (Ephesians 5:18–19; Colossians 3:16), to partake of the Lord's Supper (1 Corinthians 11:20–30), to study the Scriptures (1 Timothy 4:13), to give money (1 Corinthians 16:1–2), and to encourage one another (Hebrews 10:24–25), what advice can you give me as I try to convince them God is real and He deserves to be praised and worshipped? Signed: I'm a Television Christian and an Internet Worshiper

A: Dear I'm a Television Christian and an Internet Worshipper,

The church is made up of imperfect people who are striving to live for Christ and lose themselves in worship. As we surrender who we are to who God wants us to be, we are transparent, vulnerable, and open to the ministry of presence. This level of communion with God and community with others is not achieved at home watching television. Through a corporate experience we connect with God and other believers and witness the impact our love for God has on other people and their love has on us. Good things happen when we come together and assemble as a body of believers. Since you profess to be a Christian, you will want to obey the Word of God found in Hebrews 10:24–25: "And let us consider one another to provoke unto love and to good works: Not forsaking the assembling of ourselves together, as the manner of some is; but exhorting one another: and so much the more, as ye see the day approaching" (KJV).

Q: My boyfriend is six years younger than I am. He is very mature and grounded in the Word. We met while I was attending seminary. His sister was my dorm mate. He asked me to marry him. Although he loves the Lord and attends church, I cannot imagine him as the spiritual head of our household. I know far more about the Bible than him and we already struggle now as we pray and study the Bible together. We have dated for two years. Am I being unreasonable? It is not a matter of submission; he just can't lead me spiritually. Please help. Signed: Struggling with Submitting Spiritually

A: Dear Struggling with Submitting Spiritually,

If he just can't lead you spiritually, then just say no to the marriage. God has ordained the man to be the head of his household. Every husband and father is appointed to deal with God on behalf of his family. Just as Christ is the head of the church, a man is to be the head of his home (1 Corinthians 11:3; Ephesians 5:23–24). This does not imply an inferiority of wives. No man deserves headship because of impeccability, innate intelligence, or superior wisdom; rather it is simply God's ordained order. A wife may well be more highly educated, more gifted, and more articulate than her husband, but he is still to be the head of their home (Genesis 3:16 KJV). If he is mature and grounded in the Word, he will not lead you contrary to the Word of God.

Why can't you imagine him as the spiritual head of the house? Is it because you are older? If this is the main consideration, you are being unreasonable.

Q: My friends and I stole some jewelry from an expensive store. We can't wear the jewelry, our parents and friends would notice. I feel so guilty; I am not really a thief. We had to do it to be in with the popular girls on campus. Now I know it was not worth it. I am in the group and I don't even want to be with them anymore. There are so many things we are required to do that is not in keeping with who I am. I feel trapped. I don't want to disappoint the group but I know my parents would be horrified if they found out. I know that God already knows but He understands that I really didn't mean to do it. I am thinking about having someone take the jewelry back and leave it with an anonymous note or just giving the jewelry away as a gift to someone that my parents don't know so it will never come up in conversation. That will get rid of the jewelry but what will get rid of the guilt? Signed: My Bling Got Me In, What Will Get Me Out?

A: Dear My Bling Got Me In, What Will Get Me Out?

Thank God you want to get out. Start by confessing to God that you know what you did was wrong and violates His laws for how you should live your life as a young Christian woman. Then, you should speak with your parents. Tell them what you have done and how sorry you are. Who knows what your friends might want you to try next. Don't worry about disappointing a group of so-called friends who are leading you toward shame and self-destruction. You may think you can always return the jewelry anonymously by obtaining the address of the store and typing a letter of apology, or have a trusted friend or relative return the jewelry for you without providing information. That may sound good and like an easy way out, but it is not. To use either of these means would not negate the fact that you did steal it. The jewelry is also not yours to give away as a gift. The store would appreciate having the jewelry returned to them and may not punish you to the fullness of the law. You must confess and accept whatever punishment your parents and the law consider necessary. Bling bling got you in, but it will take repentance and confession to get you out.

Q: I'm 33 years old and before getting saved at 27 I lived a very wild life in front of my family. I was my mother's partying buddy, drinking and drugging and picking up men. Now I have a changed life and each time I visit my mother she brings up the old life and questions my Christianity. How do I help her understand that her old daughter is dead? Signed: No Longer a Party Girl

A: Dear No Longer a Party Girl,

Praise God you are no longer who you used to be. Try showing her in the Word of God what has happened to you to bring about this change. Use passages such as Galatians 4:22–31 and 2 Corinthians 5:17, and then respond to your mother with love and understanding. It may take her a little while, but if you are consistent in the way you live your new life, she will not be able to deny you are not the same person.

Your family members may be saved by your lifestyle and actions. It is common for people to remember and remind you of your old lifestyle. They miss the person who has been crucified. You will need to do more than just talk the talk; you also need to walk the walk. The enemy is the accuser of the brethren; he will always use your past against you. Don't fall back or be drawn away from the faith. Yes, you used to do any number of different things but you don't anymore. There will always be something or someone trying to pull you back. Remember, greater is He who is in you than he that is in the world (1 John 4:4). You are more than a conqueror (Romans 8:37). Surround yourself with believers who are strong in the faith—people who can undergird you in prayer as you visit with your family.

Q: I have been at my church for several years. I work in a department that requires a great deal of my time. The leader who was over the department quit. They made me step into the position. After working the department for several months, the pastor gave the position to someone else. She lasted a month before she quit. Then the pastor came back and asked me to lead the department. Once I got the department up and running, the pastor again promoted someone else, a person that I trained. I continued to work in the department because I believe that I am called to serve there, but I am angry that I keep being overlooked as others are benefitting from the work I have done. What should I do? It is becoming hard to look at others getting praise for my hard work. Signed: Tired of Others Getting What I Deserve

A: Dear Tired of Others Getting What I Deserve,

Have you talked with your pastor about his reasons for not giving you this position? It is apparent he believes you are capable as an interim leader of this department, why not as a permanent one? You say you are called to serve in this department—has God called you to lead in this capacity? Are you more useful as a soldier instead of a captain?

It is difficult to answer you without knowing the answers to these questions. Often, people may believe themselves to be capable of doing a certain job, but others see them as lacking perhaps the personality, persistence, or attention to detail needed. Doing the work may not be all you need in this position. Maybe you lack the finesse or people skills necessary for the leader of this department. Seek the Lord about this, and then talk to your pastor.

I remember when I worked in corporate America as a sales manager. There were great sales people on our team. These people always met and often exceeded quota. They were skilled in the capacity of sales but did not have what it took to supervise others. Unfortunately, because they were so good they were promoted beyond their level of competency. There are times when we set people up for failure by giving them the job to lead the work versus do the work—or giving them what they want versus what they need. What is it that you desire? Is it more money, visibility, and/or prestige? There are other ways to achieve what you really want besides promotion. It sounds as though you are making a valuable contribution where you are now. Your pastor seems to look to you for assistance in transition. If you want more, talk to God. He is the one who exalts. The Bible reminds us in

Psalm 75:6 that promotion is not from the east or the west but from God.

Q: I've been following two national ministries who have gone through some serious issues. How can I continue to follow them if they don't sit down and take account of what they have done and the impact it has had on people like me? Signed: Quite Confused

A: Dear Quite Confused,

First, let me say, do not follow any man or ministry, follow Christ. Pastors, preachers, teachers, evangelists, and other leaders are all just ordinary people subject to the same passions and the same weaknesses as we are. They have to fight the same devil we do and sometimes they lose just as we do. It always affects the body of Christ when leaders have issues and are overtaken in a fault. We may be grieved but should not despair, nor be ready to quit serving God. We should extend the same love and grace to our leaders as God has extended to us.

The Bible tells us that we "who are spiritual" should restore such a one in the spirit of meekness; remember that we too might fall (Galatians 6:1). We can restore fallen leaders by not sitting in judgment on them and by praying for them. Do not look at man; he can fail, and sometimes will. Just keep looking at Jesus. He is the author and finisher of your faith and He will never fail.

When a leader falls, it impacts the body of Christ, but ultimately, God is the righteous judge. We look at the outer man but God looks at the heart (1Samuel 16:7). How do we know the leader has not already examined himself and repented before God? Yes, there should be a season of restoration that goes beyond the confession of his fault. There should be accountability for every Christian—not just leaders. Let us pray God keeps us on the path of righteousness for His name's sake.

Q: My father is a well-known minister in our state. He loves everyone else but in his home, he disrespects my mother, has no time for us as children, and I know he has three outside children. Is this truly the face of God? Signed: Tired of Hypocrisy

A: Dear Tired of Hypocrisy,

This is an all-too-common phenomenon that is increasingly becoming more public: men who are called by God to minister to His people but neglect or abuse God's people in their own homes. Yes, they are men of God—even though they may be carnal, immature, or backslidden. We must obey the Bible and love them even while we hate their sin. What can we do about this? The Bible has the answer. It is clear that the character of a bishop, pastor, elder, deacon, overseer, or leader must be above reproach. The church must stand with the Bible to protect the people of God whether at church or at home. The church should particularly not allow a man to pastor others if he cannot care for, love, and protect the people living in his own home.

Prayerfully approach your father regarding your concerns with what appears to be hypocrisy. Your goal should not be condemnation but concern for the family and the many people who may be led astray by his behaviors. The

Bible says to honor your mother and father. Uphold your religious beliefs and convictions of the faith and live right before him. This is a very serious matter not to be entered into lightly. Second Timothy 3:16–17 tells us: "All Scripture is God-breathed and is useful for teaching, rebuking, correcting and training in righteousness, so that the man of God may be thoroughly equipped for every good work" (NIV). Stand on God's Word as you pray for your father. Seek God on how to approach him if you are the one God is sending to intervene.

Q: I am a college student working on a degree in law at a local university. I have a passion to speak and defend people, especially when I see or read about the injustices going on in our society. I am active in my local church and love the Word of God. My pastors believe I have a ministerial call on my life and always want me to make a commitment to go to seminary. I agree I have a call to work as a minister or missionary, yet I have always wanted to be a lawyer. How do I resolve what career to pursue? Will I know clearly what God wants for me or will I be in disobedience if I just go ahead and follow my dream to be an attorney? Signed: Student in Limbo

A: Dear Student in Limbo,

Praise God for His grace that sets us free! Deciding on a career is one of those areas of life where we are at liberty to choose. You said your passion is in seeking justice in our society. Did you believe you were called to be a minister before your pastor mentioned it to you? You are the only one who can resolve this issue with God's help. You can minister in the court of law just as well as in the temple. Go ahead and follow your dream to be an attorney. God never wastes anything; whatever you learn, He will use it to minister to others. You are only in disobedience when you know the will of God and refuse to do it.

There are times in our lives when others see things in us we don't see in ourselves. God uses these people to call forth greatness in us. The oratorical skills you have for defending others may be for defending the faith. Your calling could possibly be to apologetics. The ability to stand your ground and fight for justice is also needed for this calling as well. Spend some time with God praying about your desire and His will. My prayer for you is that His will is your desire. The Bible tells us in James 1:5, "But if any of you lacks wisdom [or direction or clarity], let him ask of God, who gives to all generously and without reproach." God wants you to know your purpose so you can fulfill what He created you to do. God wants the world to be impacted by your calling so He can be glorified.

Q: My friend was discipled for two years by a lady in our church. It was nice to see how much she grew in her walk with Christ during that time. I have another friend who took a twelve-week class on discipleship at her church. She too has grown by leaps and bounds. I know my life and lifestyle would be transformed by this type of intense commitment to my spiritual growth. However, I'm not sure which approach is best. How many models of discipleship are available and which one do you recommend? Signed: Ready to Be Discipled

A: Dear Ready to Be Discipled,

There are many models of discipleship. The one that will suit you best interests you the most and is offered by a mature believer. Paul said, "Be imitators of me, just as I also am of Christ" (1 Corinthians 11:1). He shared with the believers in Philippi, "Brethren, join in following my example, and observe those who walk according to the pattern you have in us" (Philippians 3:17). As you look for someone to disciple you, first find someone who is following Christ, whose life is fruitful, and who desires to see others grow in Christ. We usually won't stick with something we don't believe is effective or doesn't appear to fulfill our spiritual need.

A combination of the two things you mentioned might be what you are looking for. In order for our lives to be transformed, we must know the Word of God. We can't know God's Word unless we hear it and read it. Therefore, a good Bible class is needed. Many churches have classes during the week, and of course, Sunday school. You can also ask your friend about the class she took and take the class yourself should it be offered again. "Study to shew thyself approved unto God, a workman that needeth not to be ashamed, rightly dividing the word of truth" (2 Timothy 2:15 KJV).

It may also be helpful to find a mentor in the church—someone you can trust to give you sound spiritual guidance. Be realistic in your expectations of the person you choose to mentor you. Everyone has strengths and weaknesses. In fact, it is a good idea to build relationships with several people who have characteristics you admire. As you are looking for someone who can help you, also search for someone you can help.

When you are being discipled, it means someone is walking with you as Christ is being formed in you. The person who disciples you helps you know what it means to be a Christian and to walk out your faith daily. Discipleship is an intimate relationship of being known and getting to know someone else. While the person discipling you is pouring into you, then you can share what you are learning with someone else. In this way, you will learn to support other people while you are being supported. When you help others move forward in their Christian walk, it improves yours as well.

The person who discipled me met with me weekly for three years in her home and mine. We studied Scripture and I memorized entire passages. Among those were Romans chapters 6–8, Colossians 3, and Galatians 5. We also read through a series of books, including *The Normal Christian Life* by Watchman Nee; *Come Away My Beloved* by Francis J. Roberts; *Hinds Feet on High Places* by Hannah Hurnard; *The Pursuit of Holiness* and *The Practice of Godliness*, both by Jerry Bridges. She laughed with me and cried with me. She taught me to value silence as I sat still to wait on God. I now provide for other people what she provided for me as I disciple and mentor. May God lead you to the right person and the right program.

Q: Why is it that everyone feels like I should submit and obey? My parents want me to obey, my husband wants me to obey, my pastor wants me to obey, seems like everybody wants me to obey. I have a mind of my own and I hear from God just like they do. Why is obedience such a big deal to all of them? It is not like I am doing anything wrong. I am just not doing what they want me to do. Please help me not sound so rebellious. I want to get an understanding of how to live right. Signed: Live Right According to Whom?

A: Dear Live Right According to Whom?

Live right according to the Bible. It is there where I read about a woman named Miriam. It is so funny; her thoughts were the same as yours. She told her brother Moses, "I hear from God just like you do." She rebelled against the voice of authority in her life and got leprosy. Ouch! Read her story in Numbers 12, and learn how important it is to obey. We don't want you to end up in a bad situation. The Bible is a sacred book inspired by God to provide guidance to us for daily living. The more we know God, love God, and desire to be like God—holy as He is holy—the more we want to live His Word. We want to obey, surrender, and submit, although it is one of the hardest things we ever learn to do.

From childhood to adulthood, from singleness to marriage, we all struggle at some level with the idea of obedience. The way the Word of God describes it makes some people cringe. I can hear you now, saying; "What do you mean obey? I'm grown. I don't need anybody to tell me how to run my life." Oh, but you are wrong. We have such a resistance to the idea of obedience that we even remove the word from most contracts, covenants, and commitments.

The Bible does not ask us to consider obeying; it commands that we obey the Lord, the Scriptures, our parents, or spouses, our employers, and the laws of the land. It is a statement of fact that we always obey God rather than man; but we are also instructed in the Word of God to obey man (when he does not violate God's Word). Many of us believe we do a good job submitting and obeying. However, we only adhere to part of the request—usually the part with which we are in agreement. But sometimes it is necessary to obey when the very act confines us, challenges us, or charges us to do something contrary to our own desires. Obey? Yes, obey!

Many believers profess Jesus is Lord of their lives. Whatever the Word of God instructs them to do, they are sure to do it. They fast and pray, visit the sick, tend to the poor, and give tithes and offerings. However, when it comes to heeding to the voice of direction or counsel from someone in authority, they tend to second-guess whether the Lord is speaking. If you find yourself in a situation that calls for prayer and fasting and possibly counseling, God may reveal the answer through His Word, the wisdom of your pastor, or the intervention of a Christian counselor. However, if you do not agree with the counsel, or it does not seem sensible to you, what should you do?

At times like this we must remember obedience is better than sacrifice. We usually seek the help of others when we are not clear on what we should do. When counsel or direction is given, we need to obey unless that counsel or direction is specifically contrary to God's Word.

Obedience is our greatest act of worship; it is our radical submission and surrender to a sovereign God. It is our surrender to God's will and God's ways. When it comes to obedience we need to look, learn, live, and love.

- Look to God, His Word, and His representatives in the earth.
- Learn from our mistakes and grow in wisdom and grace as we submit.

- Live a life that pleases God consistently and be mindful to walk circumspectly.

- Love the Lord with our whole being and realize our life is not our own; we belong to God.

Q: I am so tired of being called rebellious simply because my way of doing things is different from the people I work with in the ministry. They make me feel as if I am going against God and that is not my intention at all. There are times I just don't understand and do what I think is best according to my knowledge of the Word. I have even been told I need to take some classes to help me to "rightly divide the Word," as they say. I really do want to be in God's will and make decisions that please Him. Signed: I Am Willing and Want to Do Right

A: Dear I Am Willing and Want to Do Right,

Your decisions may not be popular among those in the world or even with other believers; however, you must learn to believe God knows your heart and He is growing you up in the ministry. I'm encouraged to hear you are willing to take classes. Every believer needs to continue studying the Word. Webster's dictionary defines the word obey as "to comply with or follow commands of; to submit or conform in action to." *Strong's Concordance of the Bible* explains that *obey* comes from the Hebrew word "sama," which means, "to hear, listen, and obey." Thus, in God's eyes, if we do not perform all three functions, we fail at them all because they are inseparable. When we're willing to listen to God's voice and obey His commands, then His promises are given to us. Many of us struggle with obedience to God because of ignorance. Others struggle because of rebellion. Some of us are simply experiencing a lack in one of the following areas:

- Information – we do not know what to do.
- Instruction – we do not know how to do what needs to be done.
- Incentive – we are not clear on why we should do what is required to be done.
- Inspiration – we do not possess adequate motivation to get moving and do what we know to do.

The Bible is our guide so there is no need for us to live in deficit or doubt. When we lack information we should refer to James 1:5: "If you don't know what you're doing, pray to the Father. He loves to help" (The Message). When you need instruction you can always turn to Scriptures. The Bible reminds us in Romans 15:4, "For whatsoever things were written aforetime were written for our learning" (KJV). We are also encouraged to listen to the Holy Spirit within—who has come to instruct, lead, and guide us.

If you need incentive, take a look at Proverbs 13:13: "Whoso despiseth the word shall be destroyed; but he that feareth the commandment shall be rewarded" (KJV). God always gives us a choice. "Behold, I set before you today a blessing and a curse: the blessing, if you obey the commandments of the LORD your God, which I command you today; and the curse, if you do not obey the commandments of the LORD your God, but turn aside from the way which I command you today, to go after other gods which you have not known" (Deuteronomy 11:26–28 NKJV).

When you are in need of inspiration, be mindful God himself speaks to you through His Word. According to 2 Timothy 3:16–17, "All Scripture is God-breathed and is useful for teaching, rebuking, correcting and training in righteousness, so that the man of God may be thoroughly equipped for every good work" (NIV). Remember the saints of old pressed toward the mark of the high calling, spurring one another on toward love and good deeds (Hebrews 10:24). Your pastor, a godly friend, or a Christian counselor should spur you on as you fulfill and obey God's command for your life.

In the last days, Scripture says many will "heap to themselves teachers, having itching ears" (2 Timothy 4:3 KJV). These are "ever learning, but never able to come to the knowledge of the truth" (2 Timothy 3:7; Ecclesiastes 12:12). It is because they seek to partake intellectually of what can only be appreciated in the spirit (1 Corinthians 2:14). Don't be among them. Be one who has learned to listen to the voice of the Lord and obey.

Q: I am new at the church, but I have been serving since I started coming here. I am so excited about the power of God here. The pastor and leadership team are very anointed. I am growing so much and I enjoy giving back to a church that is making a difference in my life. Recently I was called into the pastor's office because of rumors about me in the church. Much to my dismay, people I thought really liked me have been complaining about me. They think I am fake and only serving because I want their positions in the church. This is so far from the truth. I am very hurt by their accusations and that the pastor would want to hold a meeting about this. What would happen if I wanted to be in leadership? Would my motives again be questioned? Everything I have done has been from my heart. Now my heart is broken and I don't want to do anything anymore. Please help me. Signed: A Humble Servant Who Is Hurting

A: Dear A Humble Servant Who Is Hurting,

It is such heartache when we are hurt by our sisters and brothers in the church. We often expect Christians to behave differently from those outside of the church. There is an old saying that says, "People in the church are not perfect, just forgiven." The Bible admonishes us to pray for those who have hurt us (Luke 6:28).

Hopefully, your pastor called you into his office to make sure you are serving for the right reasons. Perhaps as the new person your eagerness to be involved has been misread by others. Is there one person you could approach to ask why they have this perception of you? Take their criticism as sandpaper smoothing out your rough edges. Proverbs 27:17 tells us that as iron sharpens iron, so one man sharpens another. You may feel their assessment of you is unfair, but don't let it deter you from serving the Lord with gladness.

Finally, if you enjoy what you have been doing, continue. It may be the most difficult thing to work with people who have hurt you, but as Philippians 4:7 says, "And the peace of God which surpasses all understanding will guard your hearts and your minds in Christ Jesus" (ESV). Spiritual growth often comes from conflict, but God is able to keep your heart even when it's broken and your mind even when you do not understand why something happened. Ask God to help you establish a purpose for your life and move forward despite what others think.

Q: God has been so good to me and my family. My husband is the pastor of our growing church and we are daily seeing people's lives regenerated. When we first began the ministry eight years ago, we seemed to have so much energy and excitement about the work of the Lord. Now the days just seem long and we are both too tired to really enjoy the fruit of our labor. We have wanted to ask for time off but it seems so hypocritical to say we have grown weary in doing well. The reality is if we don't get a break soon, I am going to scream and my husband is going to quit the ministry. We are overextended in so many ways and there are not enough other leaders helping us carry the load. Our three small children see us coming and going and complain about being at church all the time. I know there are others with bigger problems but I feel bad because we are literally getting sick of the ministry. My husband has headaches, neck pain, and digestive problems. He is always rushing, doing more and we never seem to catch up. What can we do to get a handle on things? Signed: Something's Got to Give or Go

A: Dear Something's Got to Give or Go,

Both things need to happen: you need to give some areas of responsibility to others and you (as well as your husband) need to go—to bed. I can imagine you must be exhausted. Ministry is very demanding but the Bible tells us the Lord gives His beloved rest, He will not give us more than we can bear, and the joy of the Lord is our strength. Everyone needs a break and some down time to replenish. Ideally this is at the end of each day (getting six to ten hours of sleep as needed); at the end of the week (when we acknowledge the Sabbath rest); at the end of the month (taking a day of solace for reflection); and at the end of the year (for a vacation). Because Christian leaders work on the Sabbath day, they need a different day to take their rest. The role of a pastor's wife is very rewarding. It is also a life of sacrifice. You give your life, your husband, and everything else to God and the work of the ministry. So balance is a must.

It is important that you and your husband be of one accord. The examples you set for the believers and non-believers should be a realistic reflection of the Christian life, not that of superheroes. You cannot do everything, and the two of you can certainly not build a church alone. As leaders it is important to walk in wisdom. People are watching and waiting to see what you do.

You have experienced the joy of seeing others come to Christ and grow in Christ. Don't undo what you have done by trying to overdo it.

Stress is defined as a number of normal reactions in the body (physical, emotional, mental, and spiritual) designed for self-preservation. Although it may seem counterproductive for your body to shut down, it is useful for defending itself against those who push beyond their limits. Stress is also awareness that harmony and balance are being disrupted. It is an indication something is of out sync. That is what you and your husband are experiencing now.

We are a society driven by extremes, pushing ourselves beyond limits. The world would applaud this behavior. But overloaded lifestyles are detrimental to our physical, emotional, spiritual, and relational well-being. God's response to this can be found in Matthew 11:28: "Come to me, all you who are weary and burdened, and I will give you rest" (NIV).

Leaders encounter problems when too many stress producers in their lives combine with little or no time to relax. We can avoid stress by serving in areas God called us versus doing what everyone else wants us to do. There are times when the members of the congregation will have unrealistic expectations the clergy tries to fill. You and your husband need personal time with the Lord in His presence and studying His Word. You also need time with one another and the children. Ask your husband to sit down with you and pray about your schedules. Talk about some of the more satisfying times in ministry. Reflect on the impact God has made through you in the lives of those you are called to serve. Consider the state of the flock. Who is mature enough to take on additional ministry opportunities that can help your husband?

As the two of you sit together, make a plan for your family. Guard this time by turning off the phones, computers, televisions, and other things that would distract you. Read the Word of God and pray together, then play together, and plan your next steps as the Lord renews you for His work. God's Word reminds us in Isaiah 26:3 that we can be in perfect peace when our minds are stayed on the Lord and we trust in Him.

Q: I have been in church since I was 6. I started a personal relationship with Christ in my early 20s. I find myself 40 years later totally disillusioned with church. It seems as if there is really no real fellowship among the members. I feel more like I am in a club rather than a member of one body. I know it's more about inviting people into the kingdom, but how do I honestly share when I know once they join our church they will just be a number on an offering slip? Signed: Where Is the Love?

A: Dear Where Is the Love?

God is love, and He told us to love one another as He has loved us. Being totally disillusioned with your church puts you in the perfect position to minister God's grace to your sisters and brothers. You can change the quality of fellowship among the members in your church, starting with yourself. You should demonstrate for the body whatever you see as missing. Treat the members you come in contact with the way you would like to be treated. List the things that make your church feel like a club rather than a church, and if they are legitimate concerns, talk with your pastor about them. Churches need tithe and offering slips and also membership numbers so don't let those things bother you.

I want to encourage you not to become weary in well doing. It is a trick of the enemy when we have been saved a while to try to stop us from inviting others into the kingdom of God. Don't let the enemy rob you of the joy of soul winning and building up the kingdom of God. Invite people to come, and develop relationships with them so they will receive the love you give. You will receive the love you give away. I would also encourage you to get involved in the various ministries of the church. Intimacy is formed as we spend time with one another. You may also want to spend more time in prayer for the church, the leadership, and the members. People and situations often look different when you see them from God's perspective.

Q: There is an extremely nice woman within our church that shouts, screams, and cries at each service. It doesn't matter if it's a Sunday or mid-week service. Some of us think it's a show, others believe she is just touched by the Spirit, yet others think she is rude because they cannot hear parts of the sermon. Should we have a committee speak to her to find out what is really going on? Signed: Can Somebody Say Something?

A: Dear Can Somebody Say Something?

She may have issues and can only express them when she comes to church. Leave her alone. It happens even at my church. A woman at a church I attended in the past was so loud she could be heard on the ministry recordings. If it is that loud everyone else already knows. Those who should address it and think it should be dealt with will. The pastor and other leaders see it too. We all have different ways of praising the Lord. Psalm 50:23 tells us, "He who offers a sacrifice of thanksgiving honors Me; And to him who orders *his* way *aright* I shall show the salvation of God."

There seem to be many conversations about this woman. Has anyone talked with her directly? There is something about all of us that bothers others. Should we turn people loose in church to chastise others? Are there mothers in the church who may be able to minister to this nice woman?

Should she be left alone? Maybe the Lord would have you minister to her after you take the beam out of your own eye. Consider sitting closer to her, passing her tissue, moaning with her anguish, and rejoicing with her in praise.

Q: I do believe but I need help with overcoming my unbelief (Mark 9:24). I'm trying to continue to walk in faith in my everyday life but find myself relying on things seen rather than having faith. How can I live more like I believe? Signed: If It Looks Like a Duck!

A: Dear If It Looks Like a Duck!

God has given all of us a measure of faith, and we must fight to hold on to it. Mark 9:24 says, "And straightway the father of the child cried out, and said with tears, Lord, I believe; help thou mine unbelief" (KJV). You need God's help to stay strong in your faith and you must cry out to Him as this father did. Our God is the almighty God and nothing is impossible with Him. Hearing and studying God's Word will strengthen your faith, because faith comes by hearing and hearing by the Word of God (Romans 10:17). You can renew your mind by refusing to entertain doubtful thoughts and replacing them with the Word of faith.

God has given us His Spirit so we can interact and understand spiritual things. His Word is spirit and life. He has given us our five senses to interact with natural things. You need to make the decision to obey God's Word every day, instead of living solely according to what you see, hear, smell, taste, or feel. The hand is quicker than the eye so we cannot believe everything we see. Looks can be so deceiving; the ugly duckling was actually a swan. You must be consistent and determined to live by faith. This will take some work, but it will be well worth the effort. When we obey God we are walking in faith and He will perform all He has promised us.

Spiritually "dry" times are normal for the Christian. Don't mistake that feeling for unbelief.

Q: Please explain to me what God meant by the word in Galatians 6:9, "Don't get discouraged and give up for we will reap the harvest of blessing at the appropriate time." I have had a hard time trusting my interpretation. When is the appropriate time? Is it when I'm down to my last and have hit rock bottom? Why must I fail before I can receive a blessing from God, or feel guilty if I do receive a blessing from God when I'm at my best? I've been obedient all my life but feel it's because of my hard work and not accepting failure as an option. Am I being cocky? Signed: No Wooden Nickels

A: Dear No Wooden Nickels,

God's ways are not our ways, nor His thoughts our thoughts. You do not have to lean on your own understanding; let the Scriptures interpret the Scriptures. God means just what He says. Do not stop helping or working or doing the right thing because you are not seeing the desired results right away. You are going to get results at God's appointed time and only He knows the hour.

In Ecclesiastes 3:1–2 we are told, "To every thing there is a season, and a time to every purpose under the heaven: A time to be born, and a time to die; a time to plant, and a time to pluck up that which is planted" (KJV). No one plants and harvests in the same season. We are reaping a full harvest based on the principle of planting and watering; however, God gives the increase. God is helping us and blessing us every day. He is not waiting around for us to hit rock bottom before He will help us. "God is an ever-present help in trouble" (Psalm 46:1 NIV). He came that we might have life and have it more abundantly (John 10:10). We can do nothing without Him. You do not have to fail for God to help you. However, you will always fail without Him.

Rejoice and thank God whatever your state. Paul learned to be content whether he abased or abounded but he always pressed on toward the mark. When you are at your best, God still has more for you.

God blesses us because He loves us, not because of any works of righteousness we have done. Never fear or feel guilty about being blessed. "Beloved, I pray that in all respects you may prosper and be in good health, just as your soul prospers" (3 John 1:2). The Lord wants to make you the head and not the tail, to be above only and not beneath if you harken to His commandments (Deuteronomy 28:13).

You ask if you are being cocky. Yes, you are. Praise God for all you have accomplished but your works do not give abundant life. You sound much like the rich young ruler in Luke 18:18–23 who had kept the law and lived right all his life. Jesus' response to him was, "You still lack one thing . . . come follow me." This is the appropriate time for you to allow God to rule and reign in your life. It is not your works but the work Jesus did on the cross.

Q: I have a friend that is very negative all the time with anything and anyone that doesn't agree with her point of view. I really enjoy her friendship but I'm afraid her negative attitude will rub off on me. The only reason our friendship has continued is because of 1 Peter 4:9 but that isn't enough anymore! Signed: Two Birds of a Feather, Difficult Flocking Together

A: Dear Two Birds of a Feather, Difficult Flocking Together,

Birds of a feather do flock together, but it does not sound like you and your friend are birds of the same breed, let alone the same feather. Yes, it is true people of the same character usually associate with one another, as do birds of the same species. I see you said birds of a feather, are you sure the two of you have the same feather? You used some strong language in your description of your friend. If what you wrote is accurate, she may still need to be saved. If she is saved, she needs to renew her mind with the Word of God. "And be not conformed to this world: but be ye transformed by the renewing of your mind" (Romans 12:2 KJV). Being negative all the time is not a biblical trait. Our God gives us hope and a positive outlook.

You do well to obey 1 Peter 4:8–9: "And above all things have fervent charity among yourselves: for charity shall cover the multitude of sins. Use hospitality one to another without grudging" (KJV). It is a wonderful passage of Scripture we must all obey. Without the charity (love) which covers our many faults and sins, we would not able to love each other.

But we must consider the whole counsel of God concerning our friends and associates. First Corinthians 15:33 tells us: "Be not deceived: evil communications corrupt good manners" (KJV). Many other passages would be helpful as you prayerfully decide how to help your friend.

Our friends will and can influence our lifestyle. We are and will become in essence like those with whom we choose to spend most of our time. Solomon expressed the same thought in Proverbs 13:20 when he said, "He who walks with wise men will be wise, but the companion of fools will be destroyed" (NKJV).

When commenting on this verse, Matthew Henry said,

Though we must be civil to all, yet we must be careful whom we lay in our bosoms and contract a familiarity with. And, among others, a man who is easily provoked, touchy, and apt to resent affronts, who, when he is in a passion, cares not what he says or does, but grows outrageous, such a one is not fit to be made a friend or companion, for he will be ever and again angry with us and that will be our trouble, and he will expect that we should, like him, be angry with others, and that will be our sin (*Matthew Henry's Commentary on the Whole Bible*, Vol. 3, p. 921).

A true friend is one who will strengthen us spiritually and draw us closer to God. "As iron sharpens iron, so a man sharpens the countenance of his friend" (Proverbs 27:17 NKJV). When a godly friend (one of the same feather) sees error in our life, she will not hesitate to admonish us. Some friends, even those who are Christians, get upset when confronted with the truth. Those who really desire to live for the Lord will rejoice in the fact that you care for their soul. "Faithful are the wounds of a friend, but the kisses of an enemy are deceitful" (Proverbs 27:6 KJV).

While we might enjoy our friends because we have similar interests and lifestyles, the real delight of friendship comes from their faithful, Spirit-led, Bible-based counsel. "Ointment and perfume delight the heart, and the sweetness of a man's friend gives delight by hearty counsel" (Proverbs 27:9 NKJV). You can be open with a friend and know their advice comes from a desire to see you grow and prosper in the Lord. Be honest with your friend; tell her how you feel. Pray for your friend that she will learn to bless the Lord at all times and praise shall continually be in her mouth. Pray she repents and obeys the Word of God.

LET US PRAY

Father, how great you are! I thank you for being so kind and compassionate to me. Thank you that you have given me a place to learn more about you and your love. Thank you for the church, the pastors, and all the members in the body of Christ. I am encouraged by them as we pray for each other. Father, your Word is truly a light for my path. It helps me to make choices that lead to life. Thank you! Lord, there are so many temptations; please help me to stay on the path of righteousness. I praise you, Lord, that you built the church so strong that nothing can destroy it, and that we are secure in you. Father, I pray for those that are not a part of your body, the church, because they don't know you and have not accepted the free gift of salvation that Jesus offers to everyone who believes in Him. I pray that you will draw them by your Spirit and add to the church those who will accept you. Lord, I pray for my family and friends that don't know you. Lord, let me be a witness in their lives. May they see a change in me daily as I continue to grow in you. In Jesus' mighty name I pray, amen!

Scripture Truth to Help You LIVE RIGHT NOW

Category: CHURCH AND RELIGION

Telling lies about others is as harmful as hitting them with an ax, wounding them with a sword, or shooting them with a sharp arrow.

Proverbs 25:18 (NLT)

No temptation has overtaken you that is not common to man. God is faithful, and he will not let you be tempted beyond your ability, but with the temptation he will also provide the way of escape, that you may be able to endure it.

1 Corinthians 10:13 (ESV)

Consequently, you are no longer foreigners and aliens, but fellow citizens with God's people and members of God's household, built on the foundation of the apostles and prophets, with Christ Jesus himself as the chief cornerstone. In him the whole building is joined together and rises to become a holy temple in the Lord. And in him you too are being built together to become a dwelling in which God lives by his Spirit.

Ephesians 2:19–22 (NIV)

And whatever you do, in word or deed, do everything in the name of the Lord Jesus, giving thanks to God the Father through him.

Colossians 3:17 (ESV)

The saying is trustworthy: If anyone aspires to the office of overseer, he desires a noble task. Therefore an overseer must be above reproach, the husband of one wife, sober-minded, self-controlled, respectable, hospitable, able to teach, not a drunkard, not violent but gentle, not quarrelsome, not a lover of money. He must manage his own household well, with all dignity keeping his children submissive, for if someone does not know how to manage his own household, how will he care for God's church?

1 Timothy 3:1–7 (ESV)

Let the elders who rule well be considered worthy of double honor, especially those who labor in preaching and teaching.

1 Timothy 5:17 (ESV)

Obey your leaders and submit to them, for they are keeping watch over your souls, as those who will have to give an account. Let them do this with joy and not with groaning, for that would be of no advantage to you.

Hebrews 13:17 (ESV)

Religion that is pure and undefiled before God, the Father, is this: to visit orphans and widows in their affliction, and to keep oneself unstained from the world.

James 1:27 (ESV)

But you are a chosen people, a royal priesthood, a holy nation, a people belonging to God, that you may declare the praises of him who called you out of darkness into his wonderful light. Once you were not a people, but now you are the people of God;

once you had not received mercy, but now you have received mercy.

1 Peter 2:9–10 (NIV)

Shepherd the flock of God that is among you, exercising oversight, not under compulsion, but willingly, as God would have you; not for shameful gain, but eagerly; Not domineering over those in your charge, but being examples to the flock.

1 Peter 5:2-3 (ESV)

Humble yourselves therefore under the mighty hand of God, that he may exalt you in due time: Casting all your care upon him; for he careth for you.

1 Peter 5:6–7 (KJV)

If we confess our sins, he is faithful and just to forgive us our sins and to cleanse us from all unrighteousness.

1 John 1:9 (ESV)

For everyone born of God overcomes the world. This is the victory that has overcome the world, even our faith.

1 John 5:4 (NIV)

Live the Word. Live Right Now Application

Select five verses about church and religion from the previous pages and complete these exercises.

Verse # 1 _____

How would you summarize this verse of Scripture?

_____

_____

_____

What does the Bible verse mean to you? _____

_____

_____

_____

Does this verse give you instructions for hope, help, or healing?

_____

As you read this Scripture verse, do you feel the need to repent, reflect, or rejoice? _____

What do you need to do differently to live right now?

_____

_____

Name at least one person to whom you can be accountable and share your decision to live right now.

_____

Name at least one person you can encourage by sharing this Scripture. _____

Verse # 2 _____

How would you summarize this verse of Scripture?

_____

_____

_____

What does the Bible verse mean to you? _____

_____

_____

_____

Does this verse give you instructions for hope, help, or healing?

_____

As you read this Scripture verse, do you feel the need to repent, reflect, or rejoice? _____

What do you need to do differently to live right now?

_____

_____

_____

Name at least one person to whom you can be accountable
and share your decision to live right now.

_____

Name at least one person you can encourage by sharing this
Scripture. _____

Verse # 3 _____

How would you summarize this verse of Scripture?

_____

_____

_____

What does the Bible verse mean to you? _____

_____

_____

Does this verse give you instructions for hope, help, or healing?

_____

As you read this Scripture verse, do you feel the need to repent, reflect, or rejoice? _____

What do you need to do differently to live right now?

_____

_____

Name at least one person to whom you can be accountable and share your decision to live right now.

_____

Name at least one person you can encourage by sharing this Scripture. _____

Verse # 4 _____

How would you summarize this verse of Scripture?

_____

_____

_____

What does the Bible verse mean to you? _____

_____

_____

_____

Does this verse give you instructions for hope, help, or healing?

_____

As you read this Scripture verse, do you feel the need to repent, reflect, or rejoice? _____

What do you need to do differently to live right now?

_____

_____

Name at least one person to whom you can be accountable and share your decision to live right now.

_____

Name at least one person you can encourage by sharing this Scripture. _____

Verse # 5 _____

How would you summarize this verse of Scripture?

_____

_____

_____

What does the Bible verse mean to you? _____

_____

_____

Does this verse give you instructions for hope, help, or healing?

_____

As you read this Scripture verse, do you feel the need to repent, reflect, or rejoice? _____

What do you need to do differently to live right now?

_____

_____

Name at least one person to whom you can be accountable and share your decision to live right now.

_____

Name at least one person you can encourage by sharing this Scripture.

_____

CHAPTER 3

EMOTIONAL HEALING

The friend who can be silent with us in a moment of despair or confusion, who can stay with us in an hour of grief and bereavement, who can tolerate not knowing . . . not healing, not curing . . . that is a friend who cares.

Henri Nouwen

We are hard-pressed on every side, yet not crushed; we are perplexed, but not in despair; persecuted, but not forsaken; struck down, but not destroyed.

2 Corinthians 4:8–9 (NKJV)

Grief and loss. Depression and anxiety. Addiction. Domestic violence and oppression. Anger. Stress and burnout. These are common to women of every hue, race, nationality, and ethnic group. Women on every continent face challenges. There is a global outcry for justice, education, and basic human rights. We have been abused and misused by others. We have lived through adultery, abortions, abandonment, and addictions. We have abused ourselves through our bad choices. Yet, we are still here!

Emotional healing is a journey women must take to experience the love, joy, and peace God destined for them. Women have the innate God-given ability to endure, to overcome, to rise again, and to surmount adversity. We have heard the voice of God and know we are called. We are gifted, anointed, and ready to experience the fullness of everything God has for us. The Lord helps us deal with the emotional drama and trauma that tries to detour us from His path for us. We want to hear God say, "This is the way, walk ye in it." We do not want to veer to the left or the right.

> **Emotional healing is a journey women must take to experience the love, joy, and peace God destined for them.**

A comforting word for emotional healing is found in Isaiah 43:18–19. Let us look at it in several versions and translations of Scripture.

- Remember ye not the former things, neither consider the things of old. Behold, I will do a new thing; now it shall spring forth; shall ye not know it? I will even make a way in the wilderness, and rivers in the desert (KJV).

- The LORD said: Forget what happened long ago! Don't think about the past. I am creating something new. There it is! Do you see it? I have put roads in deserts, streams in thirsty lands (CEV).

- Forget about what's happened; don't keep going over old history. Be alert, be present. I'm about to do something brand-new. It's bursting out! Don't you see it?

There it is! I'm making a road through the desert, rivers in the badlands (The Message).

Contrary to what the world tells us, we do not have to remember all the bad things that happened to us and relive the past over and over. We do not have to hold grudges and get even with people who hurt us or disappoint us. We do not need to stay stuck in the muck and mire. We do not have to be angry or bitter, but we can allow the things we have lived through to help make us better, and draw us closer to God.

> *The heaviness of things that happened to us in the past often weighs us down and slows us from fulfilling our calling.*

Isaiah 43:18–19 gives us a process for emotional healing. We are told to release, remember no more, and recognize the future God has for us. God wants us to identify and release unhealed hurts, unresolved issues, and unmet needs. We need to let go of past hurts, wounds, and offenses. Hebrews 12:1 says it this way: "Let us also lay aside every weight, and sin which clings so closely" (ESV).

As we choose to remember no more, we must also choose not to carry our old baggage. The heaviness of things that happened to us in the past often weighs us down and slows us from fulfilling our calling. We must consciously choose not to live the past, but live instead in forgiveness. Most of the people who caused you pain are not thinking about you. They have gone on with their lives. We hold ourselves hostage when we do not forgive. Choose to renew your mind and take your thoughts captive. When old thoughts come up, remind yourself of how God turned your situation around for your good and His glory. Then we can rejoice.

As we learn to see God and rejoice in the present moment, we embrace gratefulness. We realize God controls our lives and He is working it out. As we rejoice, we celebrate the abundant life we enjoy because Christ Jesus died for us. We rejoice as we fulfill our kingdom dream and make an impact in the earth.

The three-step process—release, remember no more, and recognize—allows us to reconcile our past, start our healing journey, and help others on their healing journey as well. Emotional healing requires life transformation (change) and spiritual formation (growth). The willingness to be vulnerable and transparent—that is, to share your story—will help you heal emotionally. So often, even though God has delivered us and brought us out, we are still in bondage to what we believe others would say about us if they knew the truth. When we are set free, we must no longer hide. Hiding is the world's way of coping; healing means we are no longer afraid. We do not have to hide.

Our continued healing comes from personal study and application of God's Word coupled with prayer, praise, and worship (private and corporate). Once we experience freedom, God wants us to continue pursuing holiness, godliness, and righteousness.

When the issues of the past have a strong grip and you are unable to shake them, Christian counseling—which provides information, instruction, and inspiration from the Word of God—is a helpful tool. Discipleship is another instrumental resource. Discipleship helps you identify the gifts of the Spirit and the fruit of the Spirit and helps you use them.

What else can you do? Many women find comfort and healing in journaling their journey—the good as well as the bad. There is something powerfully healing about putting pen to paper and sharing—if only with yourself—how you are feeling about and responding to the events of your day. The psalmist King David certainly had his share of emotions. Think about that: we actually have an intimate look at his range of feelings and responses in the Psalms, which provide us a front-row seat where we can view his anger and pain as well as his joy and hope. Simply reading through the Psalms, a chapter per day, can remind us that we are not alone in our emotional journey.

> *Do the people in your circle of influence know more about Christ and being a Christian because of how you respond to difficulty?*

You have already experienced thousands of events in your life. How have these experiences and circumstances shaped you and affected your ability to be fruitful? Charles Swindoll said, "The longer I live the more convinced I become that life is 10 percent what happens to us and 90 percent how we respond to it."

Consider what the apostle Paul had to say about the defining experiences of his life. "My brothers, I want you to know that what has happened to me has made more people know about the good news" (Philippians 1:12 WEB). Can you say the same thing? Do the people in your circle of influence know more about Christ and being a Christian because of how you respond to difficulty? Or do you respond like the world when you encounter trials and temptations? The world says you are entitled to fall apart, have a pity party, and be immature in your emotional reaction to life. People in the world want you to try their remedies for healing your damaged emotions: think positive, take a vacation, and get more money, a bigger house, another man. The world offers you everything but God as solutions for healing, but these are not options for the people of God. We must embrace God's truth.

Life happens. James 1:2–8 tells us to count it all joy. When we know God is at work, we wait on the Lord. There is a word from the Lord for every possible emotion that we can feel. God wants us to seek His face and hear what He has to say. We are still here and can share our story of God's love and faithfulness to heal us by the truth of His Word with others travelling life's journey.

Q: My friend and I are very close; we have known each other since we were teenagers and we have always shared each other's secrets. I love her and trusted her like a sister. We are saved and attend the same church. We are both married and have children the same age. We have spent a lot of time together sharing our lives. I felt safe telling her about some intimate things concerning me and my husband. She told her husband and it got back to my husband. He is so angry with me, but I am angrier with her. I keep thinking about the shame of everyone talking about my private life. Then I think about all of the secrets I could tell her husband and others about her, even though I know I will never do it. How could she betray me like that? I don't think I will lose my husband over this, just her as my best friend. I am so hurt and sad. I know I am supposed to forgive her. I just don't see how I will ever be able to do it. Signed: Too Angry to Forgive

A: Dear Too Angry to Forgive,

Holding a grudge is a sinful pleasure. All of us are on common ground as sinners in need of God's forgiveness. If we don't forgive others, we are in fact denying and rejecting God's forgiveness of us (Ephesians 4:31–32; Colossians 3:13). Sometimes we may think of just the right words to say at just the right time to make someone who has hurt us feel small in front of all the right people. But what if holding a grudge is more sinister than you think? What if the grudge is less about the other person and more about you?

The person your grudge hurts most is yourself. You may feel discounted or rejected, but don't take what your friend did as a personal assault. This is the work of the enemy to get you to open the door to sin. This is one of the times when you get an opportunity to return good for evil and stand on righteous ground. Remember, Romans 12:21 tells us that we overcome evil with good. Do not repay anyone evil for evil. Be careful to do what is right in the eyes of everyone. As much as possible, live at peace with everyone. Galatians 6:1–2 says, "Brothers, if anyone is caught in any transgression, you who are spiritual should restore him in a spirit of gentleness. Keep watch on yourself, lest you too be tempted" (ESV). You don't have to lose your friend, just forgive her.

Don't throw away years of friendship because of this offense. Matthew 6:14 says, "For if you forgive others their trespasses, your heavenly Father will also forgive you" (ESV). Forgive her because you love the Lord. Approach your friend and restore the relationship.

There are also a few lessons for you to learn in all of this. Let me just mention three. First, you should not tell things you don't want to have repeated. Second, things between you and your husband should not be discussed between you and your friends; it violates a sacred trust. Third, others have been wounded because of decisions you made. It may be a good idea to ask your husband for forgiveness and pray he is not too angry to forgive you. Spend some time meditating on these Scriptures as you prepare to forgive.

> Love is patient and kind; love does not envy or boast; it is not arrogant or rude. It does not insist on its own way; it is not irritable or resentful; it does not rejoice at wrongdoing, but rejoices with the truth. Love bears all things, believes all things, hopes all things, endures all things.
>
> 1 Corinthians 13:4–7 (ESV)

> Now if anyone has caused pain, he has caused it not to me, but in some measure—not to put it too severely— to all of you. For such a one, this punishment by the majority is enough, so you should rather turn to forgive and comfort him, or he may be overwhelmed by excessive sorrow. So I beg you to reaffirm your love for him.
>
> 2 Corinthians 2:5–8 (ESV)

> All this is from God, who through Christ reconciled us to himself and gave us the ministry of reconciliation; that is, in Christ God was reconciling the world to himself, not counting their trespasses against them, and entrusting to us the message of reconciliation.
>
> 2 Corinthians 5:18–19 (ESV)

He who covers and forgives an offense seeks love, but he who repeats or harps on a matter separates even close friends.

Proverbs 17:9 (AMP)

Be gentle and forbearing with one another and, if one has a difference (a grievance or complaint) against another, readily pardoning each other; even as the Lord has [freely] forgiven you, so must you also [forgive].

Colossians 3:13 (AMP)

And whenever you stand praying, if you have anything against anyone, forgive him and let it drop (leave it, let it go), in order that your Father Who is in heaven may also forgive you your [own] failings and shortcomings and let them drop.

Mark 11:25 (AMP)

Q: I had a hysterectomy as a result of cancer at a young age. I was informed at that time that I could never have children. This has affected my self-esteem greatly and causes me to have periods of depression. I also feel unworthy of having a relationship because it would not be fair to my partner. I feel as if I am being punished and deprived of something most women want—children. I don't consider myself to be a jealous person, but it hurts whenever I see children interacting with their mother. When I attend family functions, I always leave with a heavy heart, often crying myself to sleep. It often takes me weeks to recover. I know I should seek counseling, but counseling cannot provide me with what I want the most. I keep my feelings to myself and never discuss them with anyone. Do you feel I could ever be happy despite my being barren? Signed: Barren and in Despair

A: Dear Barren and in Despair,

Let me say I am glad you are seeking help for the emotional trauma you have had to endure over the years. Have you consulted with a doctor about the depression? If not, please do so. There are many helpful avenues open to you. You are a woman worthy of love and to be in a relationship, whether you can have babies or not. You just need to be open to sharing this information if the relationship is becoming a serious one that could lead to marriage. You are not being punished or deprived. Most women want to have children, yet there are many who will never give birth to a child. Many of these women still become mothers. When you leave your family functions let your pain drive you to do something positive, such as being a big sister or a mentor to a needy child. You will find it so rewarding when that child interacts with you as if you were his or her mother, that you will be shedding tears of joy instead of tears of pain. Yes, you should seek counseling; it will help you see and accept the fact that you don't have to be without children, and will help you acknowledge and release your emotion. Despair no longer! Your life has been spared for a purpose. There are many children who need you and would be blessed to have you in their life.

Q: I know I am being punished. I had an abortion when I was very young. I cannot talk to anyone about this. They would all be so shocked. I am an only child with good Christian parents. I never want them to know what happened to their first grandchild. They were always planning my wedding and counting grandbabies when I was growing up. I have been married ten years now and have had three miscarriages. I am so sorry for what I did. Why won't God forgive me and stop killing my babies? My husband knows something terrible is troubling me, but I can't tell him. He is a good man and I am afraid he will hate me for bringing my punishment on him. Now he may never become a father. Signed: Will I Ever Be Forgiven?

A: Dear Will I Ever Be Forgiven?

God is a God of forgiveness and He is not punishing you for having an abortion. He is loving and forgiving. God is not killing your babies to get back at you. Most women feel intense guilt when they cannot conceive after an abortion. These feelings of guilt you have are quite normal. The first step toward healing is to ask God to forgive you.

Do not allow yourself to be consumed by guilt. Who can say whether or not the baby you were carrying would have come to a healthy full term? You said you repented and asked God to forgive you. He is faithful and just to forgive. You now need to acknowledge God has forgiven you and live like a person who God loves and forgives. Otherwise, you will be miserable for the rest of your life.

Sometimes damage is done to your body as a consequence of abortion. Your miscarriages could possibly be caused by an undiagnosed medical issue. If you have not done so already, you should ask your doctor to run tests to see if they can locate the problem. They may be able to correct it, giving you the ability to carry a baby to full term.

If you did not share all the details of your life before you were married, I would caution you to pray before you bring it up now. That was obviously over ten years ago. Yes, you should be honest about something terrible that is troubling you, but don't let your guilt lead the conversation. You may end up feeling better by telling everything that happened, but leave your husband feeling worse. What will you gain from the confession? Who will be helped by having the discussion now? Talk with your doctor. Even consider talking with your pastor or spiritual leader for guidance. If you are constantly thinking about what happened, talk with a counselor who can help you work through post-traumatic stress from the incident.

A trusted website, helpguide.org, provides some good information on the symptoms of post-traumatic stress that should help you locate and identify where you are:

Symptoms of PTSD: Re-experiencing the traumatic event

- Intrusive, upsetting memories of the event
- Flashbacks (acting or feeling like the event is happening again)
- Nightmares (either of the event or of other frightening things)
- Feelings of intense distress when reminded of the trauma
- Intense physical reactions to reminders of the event (e.g., pounding heart, rapid breathing, nausea, muscle tension, sweating)

Symptoms of PTSD: Avoidance and numbing

- Avoiding activities, places, thoughts, or feelings that remind you of the trauma
- Inability to remember important aspects of the trauma
- Loss of interest in activities and life in general
- Feeling detached from others and emotionally numb
- Sense of a limited future (you don't expect to live a normal life span, get married, have a career)

Symptoms of PTSD: Increased anxiety and emotional arousal

- Difficulty falling or staying asleep
- Irritability or outbursts of anger
- Difficulty concentrating
- Hyper vigilance (on constant "red alert")
- Feeling jumpy and easily startled

(from http://www.helpguide.org/mental/post_traumatic_stress_disorder_ symptoms_treatment.htm)

If you identify with any of these symptoms, don't be ashamed to get professional help from a Christian counselor with a good reputation in this area. God did not mean for us to carry such a burden. He is our burden-bearer. But He has also given us other human beings specifically positioned to lighten our load. After all, Christians are called upon to "Bear one another's burdens, and so fulfill the law of Christ" (Galatians 6:2 ESV).

Q: I am married to a very successful preacher in our denomination. I can see things slipping in his life as he continues to make sacrifices for the growth of our church. He recently asked me what will be the cost if we keep at this pace. I know he is aware something needs to change. I'm glad he is willing to talk to me about it. I have wanted to say something before but just prayed. This is now my moment and I want to say the right thing. He is such a dedicated leader to our family and the church. I know he wants to do what will be pleasing to God but he has also been pleasing our denomination's leaders for years. The sacrifices are wearing on him. I need some hard truth that will open his eyes. Signed: Need a Word to Share

A: Dear Need a Word to Share,

Pastors do what they do because they care so much for the people. As a pastor, his responsibilities are many. There are weddings, baby dedications and baptisms, funerals, hospital visits, crises, conflicts, counseling, and administrative duties. Pastors working with people who are suffering must contend with not only the normal stress of the job, but also with the emotional and personal feelings for the suffering. When these demands are high, we tend to neglect the things we say are most important:

- We neglect God (lack of adequate study time, personal prayer, praise, worship, and fellowship);
- We neglect family (quality and quantity of time with spouse and children); and

- We neglect ourselves (rest and stillness; sufficient, unbroken sleep; daily exercise; healthy diet; fun and laughter).

Your husband needs to get away so he can reprioritize his life and his commitments to ministry. Some sacrifice is expected in ministry, but when we neglect God, our family, and ourselves, the cost becomes too great. Consider these outcomes of neglect. When we neglect God, we turn to other idols (drugs, pornography, food, television, gadgets). When we neglect our family, we turn to other people (needy women or relationships that may lead to sexual exploitation and unholy alliances). When we neglect ourselves, we turn to anxiety (depression, shame and guilt, irritability, cynicism and sarcasm). Praise God that your husband values your feedback and trusts you enough to ask for your input. Continue to pray for him and ask the Lord to give you insight on how you might share some of these things with your husband.

Q: About six years ago I had the worst year of my life. At only 46, I lost seemingly everything and everybody who really mattered to me. My parents died in a car crash in January, my husband died of cancer in March, and my then 16-year-old daughter committed suicide in April shortly after her dad's death. Everything happened back to back. We were already struggling financially because my husband had not been able to work, and then I lost my job. I could not handle it. I could not concentrate or focus. Most of my days were spent in tears. Our house was in foreclosure and I did not have the energy to fight. So here I am now

52 and I am still overwhelmed with grief. I moved from my home into my parent's house where I grew up. Signed: Still Grieving

A: Dear Still Grieving,

The loss of loved ones is heartbreaking, but your back-to-back losses are unthinkable loads of grief to bear. I cry with you in your loss.

There is no way to rush the healing. It will take the love of God and time to ease your grief. Jesus is the God of all comfort and He will help you through the storms of life. God is able to lift up your head and give you cause to hope again. We don't always understand the ways of God or why these things happen, but when they do, we must turn to God in faith, and cry out to Him. Ask God to surround you with love and restored life and try to find comfort in being in your parent's house and in the memories of your loved ones. Then wait on the Lord; He will renew you strength and one day you will smile again.

Q: I have three kids. It's very hard for me. I attend school and work full-time. My husband and father of my children is an alcoholic and just lost his job. My family has always depended on me to be there to help them when they've made foolish decisions. But now my kids are paying the price. Since I'm always somewhere helping someone else, my children are being raised by the streets. I don't have time for myself. Sometimes I just want to run away and leave them all. Please help me. I need some wisdom from above. Signed: Highway 66

A: Dear Highway 66,

You are right, you need help and so does your husband and children (as well as other family members). Don't run away. You need to stand still and see the salvation of the Lord. So, having done all you can do to stand, stand therefore. You need to be girded up in full armor and prepared for battle. Prepare to fight for your family. This will require some changes in your approach, and adjustments in your schedule. You will need to set some boundaries for your family, establish some guidelines for your children, and pray fervently for the deliverance of your husband. You need a strong support system of spiritually mature women who are grounded in the Word of God and who will be willing to faithfully fast and pray for you and your family. Your children need you during these formative years. Your school plans may need to be postponed in this season until your home life is more stable. Don't see postponing your education as giving up on your dreams; rather, consider it an investment in your future and your legacy.

You should encourage your husband to seek counsel; even if he gets career counseling, it will address other life issues as well. Drinking, unemployment, and family responsibilities will often lead to domestic violence and abuse. Don't wait for things to get worse. Your children probably do not want to be at home alone with him and need someone who is able to tend to their needs to help guide them. The streets are never a good substitute for godly parenting. The streets will not instill Christian values and principles in your children. If your husband refuses to seek counseling, you and your children still need help. It may do them good to talk out loud about what they are experiencing. Do not run away, run to Jesus. Highway 66 will not take you where you need to go; only God can and will lead you in the right direction.

Q: I'm a 60-year old woman. I had a son at a young age. I've tried my best to raise him the best way I could by providing him with the best opportunity and exposure life had to offer. However, I didn't spend a lot of one-on-one time with him as a young child and he blames me for not being there for him all the time, which has caused a strain on our relationship. My son is now a grown man but seems to not be able to let go and get past the pain. How do I express to him without causing a fight, or worse causing more damage than what he feels I already have, of the love that I have always had and still have for him? Signed: I'm Not That Same Mother

A: Dear I'm Not That Same Mother,

Go to your son and admit you were not perfect. Allow him to express how he feels without interruption. Then acknowledge his pain. Let your son know you loved him the best you knew how at the time and you tried to give him the things you thought would make a difference in his life. Even the most well-intentioned parents make mistakes. Ask for his forgiveness. It will be healing for both of you when you allow him to hear you admit your shortcomings. Your son also needs to stop blaming you for the current state of his life. Don't let his perspective be a stumbling block for you. He is not a victim. There is no room for him to be bitter; this is the time to make his life better.

Continue to love your son as he wrestles with taking responsibility for his life. Pray for your son to not only experience your love, but the love of God. As your son embraces Christ, he will be transformed and begin to understand the purpose for his life and see how things have worked together for his good. You are not the same mother, he is not the same son, but God is the same yesterday, today, and forever—a God of love, forgiveness, repentance, and redemption.

Q: One of my best friends is in an abusive marriage. I don't understand why she stays and will not let us help her. We attend a great church that offers several support programs for people in need. The pastor's wife and I have had two meetings with her about the situation. The talks were about four months apart. Recently she had bruises on her face and arms. She keeps trying to convince us that it is not that bad and we don't know him like she does. Yet the physical abuse is becoming more apparent. Is there anything I can do or say to make her leave? Help me make sense of why a college educated, stay-at-home (by choice) mom of three children would continue to live with a man who beats her. Signed: Abuse Awareness Needed

A: Dear Abuse Awareness Needed,

In order to help women that are suffering in domestic abuse situations, we need to listen to her story and not re-victimize her with our questions and innuendos. Sometimes we do more harm than good when we say things like any of the following: Why doesn't she just leave? Why would anybody in their right mind stay with him? She must like the abuse; she keeps going back!

The reasons that women stay are varied and complicated. A woman who is being abused may leave several times in her mind and actually attempt to move out more than five times before she is finally successful. Often it is dangerous for a woman to leave an abusive relationship. But there are also many other reasons that she doesn't just walk or run away such as fear, love, commitment, perception, and lack of resources. Here are just a few of the reasons women don't leave:

- Fear of greater physical danger to herself and her children if they try to leave.

- Fear of being hunted down and suffering a worse beating than before.

- Fear of negative response or lack of understanding from family, friends, police, ministers, counselors, courts, etc.

- Love. Often the abuser is quite loving and lovable when he is not being abusive.

- Love. He really does make her feel good and he knows what she likes.

- Love. Especially during the make-up phase; she remembers what he used to be like.

- Commitment. To keep the family together no matter what. Kids need a father.

- Commitment. "I swore to stay married till death do us part. I promised to stay with him in sickness and in health for better or worse. I can't just leave him because he has a problem."

- Commitment to help. "If I stay I can help him get better. No one understands him like me."
- Denial. "It's really not that bad. Other people have it worse."
- Perception that things will get better, despite all evidence to the contrary.
- Guilt. She believes that the violence is caused through some inadequacy of hers; it's all her fault and she may feel as though she deserves the abuse.
- Lack of resources. No employment or source of income.
- Lack of resources. Including knowledge of shelters, advocacy groups, or support.
- Lack of resources. Spiritual strength, wisdom, discernment, and a loving community.

What can we do when love hurts? How do we help our sisters? How can you help your friend? The ancient proverb says that a journey of a thousand miles begins with the first step. Share a copy of this book with your friend, as well as other good books on facing domestic violence. You should also share this section with your friends, family members, co-workers, community groups, and members of your congregation to help them unravel the mysteries of domestic violence. You can take a stand so that someone else can stop getting knocked down. Pray for your friend and suggest godly counsel.

Q: My friend of 26 years is a mess. She drinks too much and smokes all the time yet she is constantly quoting Scriptures to everyone around her. The problem is that she is now working with young mothers and she thinks she is relating to them with her actions. I do not want to discourage her but the disrespect is becoming obvious. How can I tell her she needs help? Her favorite Scripture is the thorn in the flesh. I cannot take it anymore. Signed: Not Just a Fair Weather Friend

A: Dear Not Just a Fair Weather Friend,

Assure your friend of your love and concern for her spiritual and natural life. Then tell her she drinks and smokes too much and her lifestyle cancels out every Scripture she quotes. Your friend needs to hear God's truth. Check with her to see if she has really received Jesus as her Savior. If she has not, share the gospel of salvation found in Romans 10:9–10: "That if thou shalt confess with thy mouth the Lord Jesus, and shalt believe in thine heart that God hath raised him from the dead, thou shalt be saved. For with the heart man believeth unto righteousness; and with the mouth confession is made unto salvation" (KJV). If she accepts Jesus, she will want to obey His Word found in 2 Timothy 2:19: "Nevertheless the foundation of God standeth sure, having this seal, The Lord knoweth them that are his. And, let every one that nameth the name of Christ depart from iniquity" (KJV).

She is blessed to have you as a friend and to have a position where she can influence the behavior of young mothers, who carry the seed of the next generation. These young mothers can follow her as she follows Christ. As a godly example of self-control and moderation, she can impart wisdom to these mothers and still be perceived as a human but not a hypocrite.

Q: My husband has a gambling problem and we have lost all of our savings, retirement, 401K, and children's college funds. I just found out there is a second mortgage on our home. He refuses to get help. I love him but I don't want to stay until he loses the shirt off his back. What should I do? Signed: Broke and Ready to Go

A: Dear Broke and Ready to Go,

Your husband is a gambler, but you must acknowledge your husband's gambling not only affects the two of you but your entire family. Gambling is a life-consuming problem that will not just go away because you show love and under-standing. Sometimes love enables or makes it easier for the gambler to gamble. You may mean well but covering for the gambler, bailing him out, cooperating with him, or telling him you are going to leave—which is an attempt to control his behavior—will not stop a compulsive gambler. I would encourage you to pray and remember Jesus came to set the captives free. Your husband may be in bondage now but he does not have to live in bondage forever. God is able. Recovery is possible. You will need to seek professional help from a Christian counselor who understands God's power to deliver. A twelve-step program may also be helpful. At this point, your lives have become unmanageable. The Lord God Almighty is the only higher power that will help you.

Q: I'm a 56-year old woman who has been married most of my life. My husband passed away almost six years ago. I had a very blessed marriage and he was the world to me.

I don't want to sit around waiting to die. My fear is I will discard my love for him by dating or marrying another man. I had a very happy marriage and I was totally committed to my husband. I understand that I have no reason to feel any guilt. But I still feel so guilty. Signed: Too Young to Get Old

A: Dear Too Young to Get Old,

I certainly agree. At 56 you are still a young woman with a lot of life left to live. What a joy and a blessing to have had so many good years of marriage. The memories you have of your husband, you will always have. Your husband has passed on; don't bury yourself as well. Get involved with friends and develop new friendships. Grief counseling may be helpful.

Do not be afraid to date again. You have fulfilled the promises you and your husband made before God. Your vow was "until death do you part." You must part at this point. He would not want your life to die with his. Come alive. You should get up and get out, live life to the fullest because life is a gift from God. Whomever you date (or eventually marry) will find his own place inside your heart. You are not discarding your husband; he is deceased. Nobody can take his place, nor should they. Your heart is big enough for more love.

What is it you are feeling so guilty about? Guilt implies you have done something wrong. Do you feel you would be cheating on your husband if you enjoy the company of another man? You may want to review your belief and what the Scriptures teach about remarriage. Are you concerned about what others may say about you moving on? Love is not replaced because you go on living, or love another person;

nor is love increased when we refuse to participate in life. The more you open your heart to love, the more love God pours into you. Loving others and being loved will keep you young for a long time.

Q: I don't know how people watch the news and listen to all that tragedy and death. It appears that we are in the last days. There are wars, natural disasters, and families turning on each other daily. I lost a close friend in the Katrina flooding and a family member in the Alabama storm. I have become so afraid of the storms. Whenever there is a strong rain I cry for hours before I finally cry myself to sleep. Signed: I Don't Want to Die

A: Dear I Don't Want to Die,

It has been said self-preservation is the first law of nature. It is a natural thing to desire life. God promised to keep us in perfect peace if we keep our minds on Him. Certainly your losses of family and friends are contributing to your hypersensitivity. God does not want us to live in fear of death or anything else. Jesus came to free us from the fear of death. We must all die, but the key to our eternal life is hidden in Christ. Put your trust in Him. He is able to keep you, even in a storm. When it rains, remember that God reigns; then rejoice in him. The Lord is the one in control of the universe, the winds and the waves obey His voice. While you are alive, live your life to the fullest. Dance in the rain, play in the snow, rest in the sunshine.

Q: I'm 30 and have two children. I've been married for ten years. My husband is a drug dealer. We have a very nice life.

I love him so much and he gives me all the love a woman would wish for. Yet I can no longer pretend that I don't know how he gets his money. I tried to convince him that this is not the life for us. He keeps telling me that the money is very good, and he has people working for him, so he claims he never sees the drugs and will never allow it around me and the kids. What can I do? Signed: Whatcha Gonna Do (When They Come for You?)

A: Dear Watcha Gonna Do?

I'm encouraged that you realize your living situation is a problem. How do you expect to be blessed in this arrangement? Open your eyes wider and see the danger. Your happiness cannot be built on harming other families. You obviously know this will bust wide open one day soon. Don't wait for them to come for you and your children. Confronting the situation will mess up your playhouse, but you may want to tear it down and rebuild before it comes tumbling down. The Word of God calls us to stand on Jesus Christ the solid rock. Your house is built on the wrong rock (crack, heroin, weed, etc.), which is sinking sand.

Your husband needs to utilize some of his other skills and abilities and get a legitimate job. I know you have tried to talk with him before, but it sounds as though things have become more intense. Jesus is the solid rock upon which the foundation of your home should be built. Take your children to church and pray for your husband. Ask God to turn your husband's heart to the Lord and to give you the grace to make the necessary decisions to walk away from what he perceives as a lucrative lifestyle.

Thank God you are not a pretender but conscious about what is going on. However, if you continue to avoid the tough conversation about making changes, you are just as much at fault as he is. Do not be afraid; the Lord is with you. Make an appointment with a Christian counselor or your pastor. You need to tell it before it is told. You and your children are not as protected as you may want to believe. Drug dealers' associates don't always respect family boundaries . . . not to mention the ongoing possibility of your home being raided by law enforcement. They won't necessarily believe you when you say that neither you nor your children played any part in the illegal activity that is swirling around you. Although you have love, there is no peace and soon you will lose your joy. You cannot cultivate the fruit of the Spirit in sin. Get help quickly by talking with your spiritual and legal advisors to consider your options to protect yourself and your children.

Q: My heart is heavy as I write to you, because I just overheard a conversation between my daughter Amy and one of her friends. Amy said her boyfriend called her a bad name and slammed her into the wall at school, because he heard she was seeing another boy. Amy said she was scared at first and then she was stunned, but Scott looked more hurt than she felt. He assured her that he loved her too much to hurt her, and he never meant to push her that hard. Then she showed her friend the bruises on her arm and on her shoulder where she hit the wall. Amy's friend gasped so loud I knew it was bad. My daughter is dating a boy that is abusing her. What steps should I take to keep her safe? How can I help her understand that this is bad? Signed: Heavy Heart

A: Dear Heavy Heart,

You need to provide your daughter with the support to deal with the pitfalls and pressures of relationships while maintaining her Christian principles. Encourage her to talk to you about what she believes to be positive behaviors versus risky ones. If she tells you herself about the incident, don't come off as judgmental. However, assure her it is never acceptable for someone to manhandle her or even verbally abuse her. Find out where she is in regard to self-esteem.

It has been reported that an alarming number of teenage girls are being controlled and abused by their boyfriends beginning as early as middle school. Often these boys come from homes where they witness verbal and physical abuse and they are beginning to perpetuate the cycle. One of the warning signs is when the young man declares his "love" early on. This declaration is made to control the relationship. He has staked his claim and she belongs to him. To most teen girls, fits of jealousy mean "he really loves me" and anything that stirs up his anger means she is at fault.

Abusers often try to isolate their partners. Your daughter needs to surround herself with friends and family members her age who share the same interests. She needs to get active in church, volunteer with organizations to enhance her high school experience, and expand her interests.

Already your daughter is making excuses for his behavior and accepting it. There is no excuse for abuse of any kind. Yelling, pushing, possessiveness, insults, and intimidation are signs of control. Your daughter needs to know abuse is a choice. She needs to end this relationship now. Everyone deserves to be respected. Remind your daughter she is precious in the eyes of God (Psalm 139:17–18). This Scriptures say God thinks about us a lot and is concerned about every aspect of our lives. Just as God loves your daughter she should love herself.

Q: My friend's boyfriend is always putting her down. He even talks about her when others are around. He says things in a joking manner, which we can all tell is very hurtful. She is not the same person she was when they first started hanging out with each other. Signed: What Can I Do?

A: Dear What Can I Do?

Don't stand by and watch your friend suffer abuse. Yes, this is classified as abuse. Anything a person says in an attempt to belittle another person is abusive. I do not know why he would behave in this way toward someone he is supposed to like and is dating. He may be suffering from poor self-esteem and builds himself up by putting someone else down. Tell your friend love is not supposed to hurt like this, and she should consider not dating anyone who hurts her or thinks so little of her. Read 1 Corinthians 15:33: "Do not be deceived: Bad company ruins good morals" (ESV). He is bad company. Not only is he bad company, he is also bad for her self-esteem. If holding on to him is so important, even though he treats her with disrespect, then she does not know who she is in Christ.

I do not know your friend's background or why she would see such behavior as acceptable. Maybe she has witnessed abuse growing up and it's all she knows. Maybe this type of behavior is okay in her other circle of friends. Or maybe she is just desperate to fit in and feel loved. Whatever the case, maybe you can help her change and see things differently. Often, verbal or other types of non-physical abuse are not considered abuse. However, consider this simple definition: Domestic or intimate partner violence/abuse is a pattern of assaultive and coercive behaviors by an adult including physical, sexual, and psychological attacks, as well as economic coercion used against current or former intimate partners.

Examples of physical abuse include slapping, shaking, beating with fist or object, strangulation, burning, kicking, and threats with a knife or gun. Sexual abuse includes coerced sex through threats or intimidation or through physical force, forcing unwanted sexual acts, forcing sex in front of others, and forcing sex with others. Psychological abuse involves isolation from others (including family and friends), excessive jealousy, control of activities, verbal aggression, intimidation through destruction of property, harassment or stalking, threats of violence, and constant belittling and humiliation

More than likely your friend will tell you her boyfriend is not like this all the time and that he really is a great guy. She may be fooled by his charm but from what you are sharing he has already demonstrated an abusive pattern of behavior. It will only get worse if she continues to allow it.

LET US PRAY

O God! I am glad you are God and you know all things. The world is so full of trouble, and my life is full of so many things. I know all of them are not worthwhile, yet I try to control and keep up with everything. Sometimes I feel like a juggler whose plates are starting to fall. I am overwhelmed by my life. I am glad I can pour out my grief and sorrows before you without fear of being judged or turned away. I am glad I can run to Jesus. Thank you for loving me even when I find it hard to love myself. Thank you for forgiving me over and over again. I would be so lost without you. In this life I suffer not only my own losses and emotional upheavals but those of my family and friends too. Father, I pray that they would receive your love and healing from depression, and relief from anxiety and stress. Please send them your peace that passes all understanding. Lord, thank you that you deliver and set free. God, I thank you that I no longer need to be bound by anything and that there is now no condemnation for those who have accepted you as Savior and Lord. God, I am so glad that old things have passed away and that I am a new person in you. Thank you that I am not defined or held back by anything that has happened to me but I am daily becoming all that you want for my life. Thank you, Lord. In Jesus name I pray, amen!

Scripture Truth to Help You LIVE RIGHT NOW

Category: *EMOTIONAL HEALING*

"Forget the former things; do not dwell on the past. See, I am doing a new thing! Now it springs up; do you not perceive it? I am making a way in the desert and streams in the wasteland.

Isaiah 43:18 (NIV)

Brothers, I do not consider that I have made it my own. But one thing I do: forgetting what lies behind and straining forward to what lies ahead, I press on toward the goal for the prize of the upward call of God in Christ Jesus.

Philippians 3:13–14 (ESV)

Therefore, since we are surrounded by so great a cloud of witnesses, let us also lay aside every weight, and sin which clings so closely, and let us run with endurance the race that is set before us.

Hebrews 12:1 (ESV)

No weapon that is fashioned against you shall succeed, and you shall refute every tongue that rises against you in judgment. This is the heritage of the servants of the LORD and their vindication from me, declares the LORD."

Isaiah 54:17 (ESV)

I waited patiently for the LORD; he inclined to me and heard my cry. He drew me up from the pit of destruction, out of the miry bog, and set my feet upon a rock, making my steps secure. He put a new song in my mouth, a song of praise to our God. Many will see and fear, and put their trust in the LORD.

Psalm 40:1–3 (ESV)

Why are you cast down, O my soul, and why are you in turmoil within me? Hope in God; for I shall again praise him, my salvation and my God.

Psalm 42:11 (ESV)

For I am sure that neither death nor life, nor angels nor rulers, nor things present nor things to come, nor powers, nor height nor depth, nor anything else in all creation, will be able to separate us from the love of God in Christ Jesus our Lord.

Romans 8:38–39 (ESV)

Blessed be the God and Father of our Lord Jesus Christ, the Father of mercies and God of all comfort, who comforts us in all our affliction, so that we will be able to comfort those who are in any affliction, with the comfort with which we ourselves are comforted by God.

2 Corinthians 1:3–4

Refrain from anger, and forsake wrath! Fret not yourself; it tends only to evil.

Psalm 37:8 (ESV)

A stone is heavy, and sand is weighty, but a fool's provocation is heavier than both.

Proverbs 27:3 (ESV)

Live the Word. Live Right Now Application

Select five verses about emotional healing from the previous pages and complete these exercises.

Verse # 1 _____

How would you summarize this verse of Scripture?

_____

_____

_____

What does the Bible verse mean to you? _____

_____

_____

Does this verse give you instructions for hope, help, or healing?

_____

As you read this verse of Scripture do you feel the need to repent, reflect, or rejoice? _____

What do you need to do differently to live right now?

_____

_____

Name at least one person to whom you can be accountable and share your decision to live right now.

_____

Name at least one person you can encourage by sharing this Scripture. _____

Verse # 2 _____

How would you summarize this verse of Scripture?

_____

_____

_____

_____

What does the Bible verse mean to you? _____

_____

_____

_____

Does this verse give you instructions for hope, help, or healing?

_____

As you read this verse of Scripture do you feel the need to repent, reflect, or rejoice? _____

What do you need to do differently to live right now?

_____

_____

_____

Name at least one person to whom you can be accountable and share your decision to live right now.

_____

Name at least one person you can encourage by sharing this Scripture. _____

Verse # 3 _____

How would you summarize this verse of Scripture?

_____

_____

_____

What does the Bible verse mean to you? _____

_____

_____

Does this verse give you instructions for hope, help, or healing?

_____

As you read this verse of Scripture do you feel the need to repent, reflect, or rejoice? _____

What do you need to do differently to live right now?

_____

_____

Name at least one person to whom you can be accountable and share your decision to live right now.

_____

Name at least one person you can encourage by sharing this Scripture. _____

Verse # 4 _____

How would you summarize this verse of Scripture?

_____

_____

_____

What does the Bible verse mean to you? _____

_____

_____

_____

Does this verse give you instructions for hope, help, or healing?

_____

As you read this verse of Scripture do you feel the need to repent, reflect, or rejoice? _____

What do you need to do differently to live right now?

_____

_____

_____

Name at least one person to whom you can be accountable and share your decision to live right now.

_____

Name at least one person you can encourage by sharing this Scripture. _____

Verse # 5 _____

How would you summarize this verse of Scripture?

_____

_____

What does the Bible verse mean to you? _____

_____

_____

Does this verse give you instructions for hope, help, or healing?

_____

As you read this verse of Scripture do you feel the need to repent, reflect, or rejoice? _____

What do you need to do differently to live right now?

_____

_____

Name at least one person to whom you can be accountable and share your decision to live right now.

_____

Name at least one person you can encourage by sharing this Scripture.

_____

CHAPTER 4

SEX AND SEXUALITY

Promise me, O women of Jerusalem by the gazelles and
   wild deer,
not to awaken love until the time is right.

                                   Song of Solomon 2:7 (NLT)

But among you there must not be even a hint of sexual immorality, or of any kind of impurity, or of greed, because
these are improper for God's holy people.

                                   Ephesians 5:3 (NIV)

Older women from my mother's era are in a unique
position when it comes to telling us how far away
we are from God's ideal of sexuality and sex in
marriage. You only have to bring up the subject of sex in
their presence to hear them say, "No way, that never would
have happened in my day."

How far have we moved away from God's intention for
our sexuality? God planned for sex to be a part of marriage;
for procreation, recreation, and stimulation. We are charged
in Genesis 1:28 to be fruitful and multiply to produce a

godly seed. In 1 Corinthians 7:5 we are reminded we are not to withhold sex from our partners but we are to come together and satisfy one another. The Song of Solomon expresses the sensually stimulating side of sex with a beloved spouse. Nevertheless, even Solomon warns us in Song of Solomon 3:5 to not awaken desire before it is time, which is the current state of our society. Lust, unbridled desire for the opposite and same sex, and fulfillment of those desires outside of marriage have become the new norm. We have moved very far from God's intent for our sexuality.

> *It is still God's intent for us to say "I do" at the altar before we alter our sexual status by engaging in sexual activities.*

It is still God's intent for us to say "I do" at the altar before we alter our sexual status by engaging in sexual activities. The Bible tells us in 2 Timothy 2:22 we should "Flee also youthful lusts: but follow righteousness, faith, charity, peace, with them that call on the Lord out of a pure heart" (KJV). All unmarried people should heed the admonishment in 1 Corinthians 6:18 to "flee fornication" or any sexual activity until they get married. "Every sin that a man doeth is without the body; but he that committeth fornication sinneth against his own body." Adolescents need to flee fast the considerable amount of information and sexual stimulation they receive through the music industry, radio, television, print media, and the Internet. With these multiple sensory assaults, it makes it difficult (but not impossible) to avoid exposure to sexuality. However, each person has a choice and we need to help our young people choose God's intent for purity.

Most of us acknowledge that hearing, viewing, or being otherwise exposed to sexually explicit materials can potentially lead to sexual arousal. I have talked with older women—the MaDears, Nanas and Big Mamas—and most of them did not become aware of the sexual differences between boys and girls until their moms, aunts, or grandmas had "the talk" with them about the birds and bees. The talk, which consisted of sexual information about procreation, was usually an awkward and embarrassing conversation, and typically took place when the girl started her menstrual cycle. Sex was not presented as enjoyable but an obligation to your husband and a necessity for having children. Sex between married people was done in the dark, and not discussed in the light with others.

Our young girls today receive many mixed messages from every direction. Instead of marriage, they are having children out of wedlock by design. They believe you need to "give it up" to get him and the more sex they give the better their chance of keeping him or getting a husband. Young girls are looking to be sexy and "freaky" based on the songs they hear. Some even believe a husband is not necessary; they equate living together as better than being married. Where do they get these messages? They certainly do not get this information from the Word of God or the wise women of Titus but from their peers, the media, and every source imaginable. The amount of sexual content on television has doubled in recent years. Teenagers are watching programs that incite them to have sex, yet give them little or no information about the consequences of sexual practices.

As a result, people do not buy into the idea of staying a virgin until marriage. Although our parents' generation may have been squeamish about sexual discussions, they had numerous adages and proverbs to help communicate their sentiments about the subject such as, "Keep your dress down, your panties up, and your legs crossed."

Where are the women who are living right? We have a responsibility to help young women develop a biblically balanced, proper perspective on female sexuality, body image, and sexual pleasure in marital relationships. Many women are selling themselves cheap: they confuse sex with love. Others have limited economic resources and they see using sex as a way of "getting over" on someone else. They do not believe using sex to get money is a big deal at all. In counseling, I have heard women say, "Well, he pays my cell phone bill. He will also pay my car note and help me out with my children on occasion. I'm getting the better end of this deal. Having sex with him is the least I could do. It's easy and it doesn't last that long. I just pretend to enjoy it so that he can hurry up and finish." Statements such as this indicate a woman has not learned to value her body. God says we are "precious and honored" in His sight (Isaiah 43:4 ESV); "fearfully and wonderfully made" (Psalm 139:14 ESV); He says that he has "loved [her] with an everlasting love" (Jeremiah 31:3 ESV).

> **God says we are "precious and honored" in His sight**

Giving yourself sexually is really the ultimate act of commitment in a male/female relationship. Young women (and older ones too) need to realize they have already been bought with a price. Jesus Christ gave His life in exchange for theirs. Your body is not your own to give away or sell cheaply. Just because someone takes you out on a date, perhaps to dinner and the theater, you do not owe him sexual favors in return. This thought seems so old fashioned now, when many young women do not date just one guy; they have a few "friends with benefits" (male or female friends with whom they have sexual activity).

I give all praises to God because He has delivered me from my sexual history. You only need to read the preface of the book *Prone to Wander: A Woman's Struggle with Sexual Sin and Addiction* (Black and Harlin, 2002) to realize I have not always been a saint living a lifestyle of holiness:

> When we first began the (book) project, we were hard pressed to remember what it was like to live a totally entangled lifestyle. Caught in a web of lies and deception; we were totally consumed by the desire for more and more. There was a void in life that we sought to fill through means that now seem unimaginable. We made choices and took risks that no one in their right mind would do. We were obviously not in our right mind, "the mind of Christ Jesus."

It may feel awkward for parents to have the talk but it is more necessary now than ever before and at a much earlier age. Our daughters need to hear our voices. The young girls who are exposed to an overabundance of sexual stimuli need to embrace the truth about God's limits, His love, and His standards. We must tell our daughters, our sisters, and ourselves God's truth; knowing God's Word of truth will be the only thing to set them free. We are made in the image of God and when the Holy Spirit fills us, then

> *We must tell our daughters, our sisters, and ourselves God's truth; knowing God's Word of truth will be the only thing to set them free.*

we are empowered to make different choices. When people think we are strange, it is okay, because we are a peculiar people. We do not think, act, or respond in the ways of the world or others who do not know Christ.

We need to provide hope, help, and healing to assist those who are tangled in sexual sin and allow God to unravel confusion, break ungodly soul ties, and restore us to the image of God. Those of us who are pastors, youth workers, counselors, teachers, and speakers need to use our platforms to speak words of life from the book of life and impart wise instruction and information for sexual purity and sexual healing. Women of God need to spend time mentoring and discipling our young women, helping our young girls in the development of their identity, and preparing them for their destiny. We need to speak up and not let them live lives leading them away from God.

> **Sex is a gift from God to married people; don't open someone else's present.**

The only safe sex before marriage is no sex. Safe sex means no diseases, no children, no emotional confusion, no psychological damage, and no spiritual dilemma. Here is a bit of advice for young and old: sex is a gift from God to married people; don't open someone else's present. Our voices need to be heard loud and clear as we represent the voice of God's truth regarding sexuality. Abstinence, adultery, pornography, sexual addiction, impotence, frigidity—these are key areas of sexuality where women have questions and need truth from the Word of God. Let's take a look at the questions that touch on these issues.

Q: I have been betrayed in the worst way; my sister had an affair with my husband. They have a child together. My mother knows my nephew is my husband's child. She assumed I knew. My nephew Burt is ready for college and my mother asked me if his father would be able to help. I said, "How would I know?" She responded, "Ask him. We never asked you all to help before because you had small kids. So we helped your sister raise Burt. But now that your financial situation has improved, we could use a little help." I never answered her. I had to get out of there before she saw my face. I went home and cried, screamed, and had a meltdown. My husband and my sister slept together twenty years ago and I never knew it. The sweet little nephew I helped raise along with my kids actually had the same father. There are so many thoughts in my head it feels as if it is going to explode! My life has been a lie! How could they live this lie and how could they lie to me all this time? Signed: Ultimate Betrayal

A: Dear Ultimate Betrayal,

It is, indeed, the ultimate betrayal for your sister to have an affair with your husband. I can only imagine how painful it is to hear this revelation. I'm sure it must be mind boggling and hurtful that they kept the truth of your nephew's paternity from you for so many years. You should discuss the request made by your mother with your husband immediately. Your mother is likely to bring it up if you don't. It seems your sister has carried this as long as she plans to without assistance. Since your husband is your nephew's biological father, he does have an obligation to help in any way possible with his education and needs. Having a discussion with your sister, while it may be challenging, may also provide needed healing. God will help you sort through all the many emotions you have about each relationship.

You, your husband, and sister should meet and discuss what is in the best interest of your nephew—who is innocent in all this. Now that the issues are being discussed, it may be wise to include your nephew, since he is of college age. He has a right to know what's going on. Forgiving your sister—and your husband—is another step you should take. Holding anger and animosity will only destroy you. Although it is an unfortunate situation, the situation will not change and must be dealt with in a positive manner. There should also be a discussion with your children, depending on their ages. Secrets can only hurt and foster a continued atmosphere of distrust. Sin does complicate things but God's grace heals old and new wounds.

As you probably are aware, adultery is biblical grounds for divorce, but not a biblical mandate. Prayerfully consider, with the help of counseling, whether you will stay in the marriage.

Q: My husband and I have been married for 15 years. We are both Christians, committed to the lordship of Jesus Christ. Lately our intimate life has spiraled downward. We have sought godly counseling from more than one person. The overwhelming response has been, "the marriage bed is undefiled." So I guess this is supposed to mean whatever we do is up to us. It's been said that it's okay for us to experiment with pornography and toys in the privacy of our bedroom. Is this true? Signed: The Ups and Downs of Porno

A: Dear Ups and Downs of Porno,

As Christians committed to the lordship of Jesus Christ you do not need to guess about what the Word of God means. It is true the marriage bed is holy and undefiled, but pornography is not. Experimenting with pornography is as dangerous as playing with fire; they both can get out of control. Remember, your intimate life consists of more than just the marriage bed. When your private, personal time is affected, it is usually an indication of a breakdown somewhere else in the marriage. A close personal relationship is not formed by playing sex games, but by really communicating with each other in a caring and sensitive way.

Although the Bible does not address specifically pornography, in Matthew 5:27–29 the Scriptures say if anyone looks at a woman (or man) with lust, he has already committed adultery in his heart. Pornography is used to elicit lust. Are you okay with your husband committing adultery? Would he be all right with you doing so? In viewing pornography you are participating vicariously in the acts presented.

Ephesians 5:3–5 tells us fornication, uncleanness, and covetousness (desiring something that is not yours) should not be found among the saints. Furthermore, people who do these things will not inherit the kingdom of God. Verse 11 goes on to say saints should have "no fellowship with the unfruitful works of darkness, but rather reprove them" (KJV). Pornography is obsessive and pervasive by nature; it leads to idolatry. Pornography provides the stimuli and the rituals worship sexual immorality rather than God.

Realistically, marriages cannot sustain the passion and excitement of newlywed life. Careers, children, finances, and many other aspects of life can put a damper on relationships. However, you can regain some of the passion and create new exciting experiences by changing your attitudes and putting forth some extra effort. There are many Christian marriage seminars that can be extremely helpful. Find one and attend. Marriages need maintenance. Invest in your marriage with date nights and romantic weekend getaways. Remember what made the two of you fall in love and re-create those experiences and encounters. Spend time talking to one another instead of reacting to your daily routines. Do not take each other for granted and make each other the priority. Finally, let me be very clear about pornography: there is no "up" side to porno.

Q: I feel terrible. Just the mere thought of it makes me feel like a horrible person. My husband has not been able to perform in bed, and I told him it does not matter. But to be truthful it does. If I cannot turn my husband on, what kind of woman or wife am I? He said he just has a lot on his mind but he refuses to share with me what it is. I know I have gained a little weight over the years and I have been trying to lose it but it is taking longer than it has in the past. I believe he no longer finds me attractive. I have seen the way he looks at other more attractive women when he doesn't think I am watching. I am afraid I am going to lose my husband. What should I do? Signed: Weighed Down

A: Dear Weighed Down,

The measure of a man is not in his ability to perform the sex act. Any animal can do that, even the birds and bees do it. A marriage is made of more than sex. It may be just as your husband said. Try to communicate with him about his concerns. You said his impotence bothers you because it makes you feel like less than a woman. If you are feeling insecure and unattractive, take steps to change things. When we feel our lives are out of control we become fearful and suspicious and, as a result, we often misinterpret what we see. You can continue to assure your husband of your love for him and keep trying to open the lines of communication. Lose weight or do whatever it takes to restore your self-esteem. Just remember beauty is as beauty does. Keep doing beautiful things for yourself and for your husband.

There are and will always be lots of pretty girls and women who are very shapely: long legs, curvy hips, and more. These are not the things that keep a husband happy or keep him at home. According to Proverbs 31:30, looks will fade and charm is deceptive. Let your godly character and demonstration of genuine love, respect, and regard guide everything you do for you and your husband.

Q: I have a friend who doesn't claim to be a Christian. She's nice and generally a good person. She has two children ages 4 and 12 whom she loves. She is a stripper and makes more than a thousand dollars a night for her performances. She is in high demand and insists that there is no sexual activity with clients. I work making twelve dollars an hour and I'm in school. She laughs because I talk about the abundant life Christ died for me to live. How can I witness to her? Signed: Her Stripping Versus His Stripes

A: Dear Her Stripping Versus His Stripes,

Your friend is not able to appreciate the stripes of Christ yet; she is blind to spiritual things and cannot understand them. Everyone has a need in their life. She may have lots of money, but there are other areas in her life to which you can witness. It's like going against someone in battle; you look for their weaknesses. In fact, you are in a spiritual warfare. Your friend's soul is at stake.

The life your friend lives is one of darkness. Her lifestyle and questionable career choice put her life in danger. She is exposed to those who are smoking, drinking, and being sexually enticed. She is their fantasy and, although she may be saying no to sexual activity verbally, her sexually suggestive movements say yes whenever she is on stage. Clients sometimes have difficulty distinguishing that the behavior of exotic dancers is just an act and not something they really want. I'm pretty sure this is not the job she would want her children talking about at school. Nor does she want what she does in the dark of the night discussed during the light of day. God has shown her mercy and grace and given her room to change her ways.

Those who are not saved are often motivated by money and have no shame regarding their behavior. Pray that the Lord pricks her heart and moves on her conscience. There is a point when we can all see, really see, God's truth. When you are given the opportunity, make sure you are prepared. Witness to her in love and do not be judgmental or argumentative. Remember, you can lead her to the water that satisfies the longing in her soul, but you can't force her to drink it.

One more thing . . . it is amazing that most people believe in the concept of heaven and hell whether or not they live right. Ask your friend if she believes in God and eternal life. If she believes, then ask her if she thinks her lifestyle is in agreement with this concept. Hebrews 9:27 clearly tells us, "And inasmuch as it is appointed for men to die once, and after this comes judgment." Judgment is certain and she needs to make a decision about her eternal destination. Furthermore, the Scripture goes on to explain in verse 28, "So Christ having been offered once to bear the sins of many, will appear a second time, not to deal with sin but to save those who are eagerly waiting for him" (ESV). In other words, Jesus is coming back for those who are waiting for Him by living according to His commandments.

The most powerful witness you have for your friend is your lifestyle and the love and contentment she sees in your life. Just continue to love her, pray for her, and let your life be a living witness before her.

Q: I have been married for six years. I believe my husband loves me but he doesn't want to spend a lot of time with me. He never compliments me, and he is very stern. I'm lonely far too much for my comfort level. Truth is, I am very uncomfortable with the amount of time on my hands and how love starved I feel. I know that having an affair is sin. Please don't quote me Scriptures about adultery in my heart. I have been tempted to peek into pornography since this will not be hurting anyone. Some of my Christian friends have encouraged me to do this and just take care of myself. If I only watched one video a month, would that be okay? Signed: Just Want a Little Attention

A: Dear Just Want a Little Attention,

Has your husband changed since you have been married, or was he always stern and short on compliments? If you believe your husband loves you, start to build the relationship you want with him on that fact. Let him know you want to spend more time with him; plan something for the two of you to do together. I am glad you know an affair is out of the question so I won't quote those Scriptures. I will, however, encourage you to read them as a reminder of God's truth, which you already know.

Pornography is like a monster. If you let a little monster live in your house, he will grow up into a big monster you will not be able to control. No, it is not okay to watch one porno video a month or to take care of yourself sexually. Please give me some liberty, because it wouldn't be right if I didn't give you at least one Scripture about God's take on sexual immorality. First Corinthians 7:2–5 says,

> But since sexual immorality is occurring, each man should have sexual relations with his own wife, and each woman with her own husband. The husband should fulfill his marital duty to his wife, and likewise the wife to her husband. The wife does not have authority over her own body but yields it to her husband. In the same way, the husband does not have authority over his own body but yields it to his wife. Do not deprive each other except perhaps by mutual consent and for a time, so that you may devote yourselves to prayer. Then come together again so that Satan will not tempt you because of your lack of self-control. (NIV)

I am taken aback that your Christian friends would advise you to watch pornography. Seek additional counsel from someone you trust not only to give you supportive answers and the answers you want to hear; but who will also give you truth according to the Bible. Jeremiah 2:13 says, "For my people have committed two evils: they have forsaken Me the fountain of living waters, to hew for themselves cisterns, broken cisterns that can hold no water." Be careful not to drink from an unclean source that will not satisfy. Do not allow other people's opinions to influence your choices when you know what they say is not biblically based. You should always obey God rather than man.

Q: What is a mother to do when your child tells you she is gay and has been for a long time? My 15-year-old daughter shared with me that her friend is more than just a girlfriend. It was too much for me to hear that there are five of them that do sleepovers and have sex. I was aghast and did not want to discuss the matter. These girls ranging in age from 13 to 16 have been in my house. I wonder why she even told me. What does she expect me to say and what am I to do now that I know? Signed: At a Loss

A: Dear At a Loss,

Your daughter expects you to be her mother, tell her when she is wrong, and help her clean up the mess she has made of her life. I understand this was a traumatic wake-up call for you, but just imagine the turmoil she is experiencing as she tries to navigate the waters of her sexuality. At 15 she is just exploring her sexual feelings. She told you because she is confused and screaming for help! Please share your wisdom and understanding with your daughter. Help set some guidelines for her.

The fact that there are five of them (an odd number) and they are not couples means they are a group of young women playing with fire. This behavior is very prevalent among girls your daughter's age. Many girls engage in homosexual activity out of pressure and bullying, others just to fit in. It is important for you to affirm your daughter and highlight who she is in Christ. This phase of sexual exploration often passes. She is telling you either because she wants your approval or to shock you into action. Either way, you are now involved.

Seek professional counseling—for yourself to help you handle the situation and for her if she is willing to go. You can also seek support from groups and organizations that work with parents of children with sexual identity issues. Whatever you do, keep the lines of communication open between you and your daughter. Don't turn her away; it will do more detriment than good. It may have been hard for her to come to you. Don't call her names or make derogatory statements. Don't blame yourself. This is not about you. Don't get on your soapbox or break out your holy oil. Just pray with your daughter, for her, and for strength as God moves.

Q: I'm the first lady of a large inner-city church. My husband has been unfaithful with women in the church. Everyone knows it and laughs at both of us on Sundays. My hat is not big enough to cover my shame. I really love my husband and plan to stay with him. I want to be an example to the younger women in the church of how to make it through challenging times. Please help me address this issue. Signed: Sounds Silly but I'm Staying

A: Dear Sounds Silly but I'm Staying,

The issue of infidelity in the church is more widespread than we would like to admit. But suffering in silence is not the answer. I think it is time for issues like this to be exposed to the light of God's Word. You have done nothing to be ashamed of. It seems, however, that your husband has been unfaithful with more than one woman in the church. The goal here is confession, repentance, and restoration—not condemnation. So many families end in destruction because of unfaithful men of God, and, yes, women of God too.

The Bible permits divorce after infidelity, but I believe God wants to see reconciliation—regardless of difficulties. Infidelity is more than a difficult problem in marriages; it breaks the marriage covenant with God—who never breaks His covenant with us, even when we are unfaithful. In view of this, as Christians we should—but are not biblically required to—maintain our marriage covenant with an unfaithful partner. You said you are planning to stay. I hope this means he repented and turned from this destructive sin.

Since people already know about your husband's indiscretions and are laughing and talking behind your back, the two of you should take control of the situation. You both should talk openly about your husband's fall from grace and about how God has given you more grace as his wife to enable you to forgive him. Tell the members of your congregation God will also give them more grace to forgive and to pray for you and your husband. What a wonderful example this would be for the other couples and young women and men in your church. This should be done together in a class or group setting, not one on one, which can lead to more gossip. I recommend that you read *Warning to Ministers, Their Wives and Mistresses* written by Dr. Betty R. Price.

Finally, on a practical note, make sure that you are both tested for sexually transmitted diseases, including HIV. It's not pleasant to discuss, but it is better to know than not.

Q: Can Mr. Right be right now? I'm a 39-year-old single woman who has been celibate for the past two years. I attend church, tithe, serve in ministry, am active in my community, and have lived holy. These past few months have been very lonely. I recently met someone who is saved and a nice guy. I'm tired of being alone and I miss the physical contact. How do I tell him I want and need to get married right now? Signed: Celibate Two Years and Counting

A: Dear Celibate Two Years and Counting,

The Bible says He that finds a wife finds a good thing (Proverbs 18:22). I never read in the Word of God where a woman finds a husband, let alone tells him, "I want to marry you and need to marry you right now." You gave a list of all the things you do for God but never mentioned your love for Him or your relationship with Him. Your holy living seems to be done out of duty, which can be tiring. You seem to imply the least God could do for you in return is give you a husband right now, because you have suffered celibacy for two years and that's long enough. Focus on your spiritual life. You have met someone; don't chase him away by being pushy and needy. Enjoy the companionship and let the relationship develop naturally. If he is the one, God will let him know that he has found his good thing. Remember,

God is with you and you are never alone, even in singleness and celibacy.

Q: I have been married 15 years and my husband and I love each other, but our sex life was dull. My husband suggested we look at an X-rated movie together. It was okay for a while, but I started feeling less desirable when I saw my husband responding to the images of other women better than he did to me. After I complained, he stopped watching them, but now I am watching them a lot and am not as interested in being with him as I was before we watched the pornography. What can I do to change things? Porno has wrecked my marriage! I can't stop fantasizing about every man I see and wondering if he would be like the video. I know that I am in danger. Most of my time is now spent thinking about how I would get away with doing something with someone else and not getting caught. What I see on the screen is no longer satisfying. Please help me. Signed: Before I Go Too Far

A: Dear Before I Go Too Far,

Porn can become an addiction. It can impact a person's entire life: their money, ambitions, time, commitments, and yes, even their closest relationships. Porn carries the message that it is all right to commit adultery—to desire and lust for someone other than your mate. The clock is ticking and every second of every minute of every hour of every day someone, somewhere is sneaking a peek at pornography.

So often we hear about men and their struggles with lust, adultery, sexual addiction, and other sexually deviant behavior, but the reality that women suffer too has been largely ignored, especially in Christian communities. The activity of women is not as blatant or obvious and does not indicate the intensity of the problem or the level of exposure women have to sexually explicit literature, photography, and activity. Pornography is big business and a much bigger problem than most of us realize.

Even with all the women I have counseled who dealt with this issue I was surprised by the findings and the statistics. Porn revenue is larger than the combined revenues of all professional football, baseball, and basketball franchises. US porn revenue exceeds the combined revenues of ABC, CBS, and NBC. The pornography industry is larger than the revenues of the top technology companies combined: Microsoft, Google, Amazon, eBay, Yahoo!, Apple, Netflix, and Earthlink. The 2006 top search requests were for sex, adult dating, adult DVD, porn, sex toys, free sex, cybersex, sex chat, xxx, and nudes.

Pornography rules the Internet. Over 12 percent of websites (4.1 million) are related to porn. Approximately 25 percent (68 million) of the total search engine requests are for pornographic material. Daily pornographic e-mails number at 2.5 billion, which accounts for 8 percent of all e-mails. When considering pornographic web pages listed per country, the US has over 95 percent of all web pages (244,661,900) compared to Germany (10,030,200). Is pornography a problem? Absolutely. Every second, minute, and hour thousands are being spent on pornography, thousands of Internet users are viewing pornography, and new pornographic videos are being created in the United States. Men and women struggle with this destructive addiction.

I assume you are a Christian. If so, the Bible says in 1 Peter 4:3, "For the time that is past suffices for doing what the

Gentiles want to do, living in sensuality, passions, drunkenness, orgies, drinking parties, and lawless idolatry" (ESV). We are called by God not to return to unrighteous, reckless living and sexual perversion. Furthermore, as you have said, it is so easy to get caught up in the sexual immorality of the world. The Bible tells us in 1 John 2:15–17 that we are not to "love the world or the things in the world. If anyone loves the world, the love of the Father is not in him. For all that is in the world—the desires of the flesh and the desires of the eyes and pride of life—is not from the Father but is from the world. And the world is passing away along with its desires, but whoever does the will of God abides forever" (ESV). Desires of the flesh will destroy you. Since technology makes it so easy to sneak a peek without anyone knowing, we feel our actions are harmless. Nevertheless, God knows every action we think we do in secret and we are admonished not to grieve or bring sorrow to the Holy Spirit by our actions. (Ephesians 4:30).

Q: I am 25 and have abstained from sex. I have always considered myself to have good morals and would like to save myself until marriage. However, I want to have children soon and most guys I date want to have sex by the third date. My family and close friends ask me often if I am a virgin still and snicker when I tell them yes. They also make references to my not liking men and being gay. This is very hurtful and causes me to cry a lot. My friends make jokes about me and have tried on several occasions to convince me to have sex for the sake of having it. They have gone as far as to give me names of guys who would love to break me in. Although I want to wait until marriage, the pressure is sometimes unbearable. As a young woman I experience the need to be sexually active at times, which is a problem within itself. I sometimes wonder if my desire to abstain from sex is the way to go. Signed: Hopeless in Savannah

A: Dear Hopeless in Savannah,

Yes, abstinence is the best way to go when you are not married. The Bible tells us to flee fornication. Read 1 Corinthians 6:18. Yes, that's right, run from fornication because it carries the seed of destruction and defiles the body. Experiencing the need to be sexually active at times only means you are normal. Do not let anyone pressure you into becoming sexually active, not even yourself or your desire to have children. People will often laugh and make jokes about things that are out of their reach or because they do not have them—like your good morals. Think about "The Fox and the Grapes," one of the traditional Aesop's fables, in which the fox covets the inaccessible grapes. Twenty-five is still young; you have many childbearing years left.

Q: I will soon graduate from college with my master's degree. I am ashamed to admit this, but I have been involved with pornography since I was a freshman in high school. Many of my girlfriends had sex party sleepovers. It all seemed so harmless, and it was fun to gather and watch movies all night. Afterward we would discuss the video as well as talk about what we would like to do with the boys at school. I accepted this weekend activity as normal until I graduated and went to college. I consider myself a good girl. I am still a virgin, and I never allow the boys to feel on my body. But after watching porn with my friends I started having strong sexual desires, and now I am masturbating 3–4 times per week while looking at porn on the Internet. The problem started after I got saved at a concert as an undergrad. Now I know this is wrong and I should stop, but I can't. I feel so dirty and guilty afterward that it is affecting my social life and my grades. I am angry with my friends for exposing me to pornography on cable. I really believed it was harmless and fun. Well, the laugh is on me as I cry myself to sleep after watching porn and masturbating. Signed: This Is Not Fun

A: Dear This Is Not Fun,

You are right; being imprisoned is no fun. You were exposed to and captured by porn before you knew it was a problem. Now that you understand and want to be free, there is help for you. Turn to the Word of God. A lot of times when people are engaged in pornography, they pull away from God because they cannot imagine God still wants to be with them and loves them. I want to expose you to the truth. God loves you in spite of what you have done. God has always loved you and He will continue to love you.

God is longsuffering. Expose yourself to His grace and mercy; it has nothing to do with whether or not you deserve it. The truth is none of us deserve God's grace, but it's freely given, and it is a gift of God. All we have to do is repent and receive that gift. God gives us plenty of room for repentance; He desires to see us change. He's waiting for us to desire to live for Him in accordance with the Word of God.

"No temptation has seized you except what is common to man. And God is faithful; he will not let you be tempted beyond what you can bear. But when you are tempted, he will also provide a way out" (1 Corinthians 10:13 NIV). Millions of women are being led astray by sneaking a peak at pornography. There is hope and help for you. You have taken the first step by acknowledging what's going on in your life. Now get help to address the issue and apply biblical principles that will set you free. You will have the last laugh. The enemy cannot hold you hostage. Jesus died for you to live in freedom.

Q: My husband used to struggle with pornography before we were married eight years ago. He blamed me because I would not have sex with him before marriage. It was a decision I made after having two children already out of wedlock. He would remind me that I had sex before so he did not understand why I would not have sex with him. We got through it and I thought everything was okay until I recently found a men's magazine in my 12-year-old son's room that was addressed to my husband. All these years of marriage I have never seen that magazine in the mail. To make matters even worse, my husband and both sons, ages 8 and 12, like to watch women wrestling, dancing, and all the shows in which the women wear skimpy or sexy clothing. We also have cable; there is no telling what else they may be watching. I don't know what to do or if I should do anything at all. Signed: Wanting to Cancel All Subscriptions

A: Dear Wanting to Cancel All Subscriptions,

This all boils down to whether or not you and your husband are Christians. The greatest factor in combating any addiction is to come under the authority of Jesus Christ. The plan of salvation requires you to confess your sins, repent, and surrender your lives to Christ. Without salvation, you cannot overcome the binds of sin. Paul wrote, "Wretched man that I am! Who will set me free from the body of this death?" (Romans 7:24).

Right now you may feel helpless in dealing with what is going on with your husband and your sons; however, the Bible tells us a sanctified wife sanctifies her unbelieving spouse (and children). This means your family falls under the umbrella of blessing and protection afforded the believer. Therefore, it is important for you to fast and pray for your family. Ask God to deliver your household from the sin of pornography.

Are your sons in church, attending Sunday school and involved in activities? Are you setting an example and teaching them about God's design for their lives? You may not be able to sway your husband away from pornography, but you have a responsibility to warn your sons of the dangers. Ask God to allow what you say to them to fall on fertile ground.

Now that you know what is going on, you cannot ignore it or pretend it is not a problem. Talk to God about how to talk to your husband. These activities are not acceptable for your husband or your boys. Don't believe the hype of the world that "men will be men." The converse is actually true: "God will be God," and He will not be mocked. God sets standards for holy living and for raising children as godly seed. As parents, you are to protect your children from evil, not expose them to it. You have a responsibility to guard their hearts and minds with all diligence.

Q: My boyfriend and I have been dating for over six months and we've abstained from sex. I'm not a virgin, but my boyfriend is. This is the hardest thing that I've had to do in my life. We are both saved and truly trying to live our lives according to the Bible to make sure this is what we both want. He has asked me to marry him. Because I have had sexual relations with one other person, I am a little experienced when it comes to my sexual desires. What should I do if it's not up to standards after we get married? Is it wrong to want more if it's less? Signed: Can I See the Car Fax Please?!

A: Dear Can I See the Car Fax Please?!

Can I see your diploma in "I am an expert in sexual standards"? According to your letter, you have not earned one. Your sexual experience with one boyfriend will be totally different than your sexual experience with your husband. There is no comparison. You and your husband will set your own sexual standards and learn how to please each other together. I know it is hard for you, because you have awakened your desire before its time. God will keep you if you obey His Word.

Read 1 Corinthians 6:18: "Flee fornication. Every sin that a man doeth is without the body; But he that committeth fornication sinneth against his own body" (KJV). I thank God you are both saved and want to live in a way pleasing to God. Read 1 Thessalonians 4:3: "For this is the will of God, even your sanctification, that ye should abstain from fornication" (KJV). These Scriptures, and the surrounding verses, will encourage you both to abstain from sex until you are married. It is not wrong to want more. Just remember what you had was sinful; what you are preparing for is bliss. Don't highlight this one experience as anything special; it was carnal. You still have a lot to learn about sex and even more to learn about the joys of this union when coupled with love and intimacy between those sanctioned by God.

Q: My husband and I have been married for eight years. He is a gentle lover who spends time talking to me, caressing me, and engaging in extended foreplay. He struggles with the idea that eight years later sex is still very painful for me. As a virgin bride it was initially acceptable but the pain has not ceased. My doctor has told him there is nothing physically wrong with my body but the problem is in my mind. I agree. In my mind I know that I was not a virgin when we married. I just didn't have the heart to tell my husband that I had been raped twice; once in elementary school and then in college. The second time was worse; it was someone I know. He kept trying to make me want him sexually even though I repeatedly said no. I want to be close with my husband and truly intimate. Should I take the risk of telling him what happened? Signed: Wanting Sex with No Pain

A: Dear Wanting Sex with No Pain,

You are right; telling him will be a risk. However, not telling him has also caused a series of problems for you and the marriage. I would advise you to pray and seek the face of the Lord prior to making any decision. Neither will be easy and both can potentially have consequences as well as rewards. If you want sex with no pain, you need to remove the painful memories inhibiting you from true sexual freedom.

The goal in marriage is to be transparent and vulnerable. We need to reveal our wants, desires, dreams, fears, concerns, and hopes for the future to our mates—not conceal them. It is difficult to be in an intimate relationship with someone who makes it a practice to provide limited information about the real person—who they are, where they have been, where they are going in life. To conceal means "to keep from being seen, known, found, observed, or discovered; to hide." The very definition sounds cold and distant. Concealing anything from your spouse defeats the purpose of marriage, which is to know and be intimate with each other so that the two become one.

Marriage is to be a source of joy and happiness in a close relationship for life. One of life's greatest joys is to be loved, known, understood, and accepted for who we are. But to achieve this intimacy, we must be honest and open. We must reveal and share our weaknesses and our strengths. As we learn to trust each other with our fragile egos, and we treat each other with respect and tenderness, we grow closer. There are times in a relationship when things done in the past are best left behind. If you find your past impacts your present or you worry about your past being revealed, it is best for you to find a way to tell it. Many people live in fear of their spouse leaving them if they find out certain things. This apprehension keeps us from being close and trusting in our loved ones.

Q: I am recently engaged. Now that I've accepted my Christian boyfriend/fiancé's proposal of marriage, we have decided together we don't want to have any children right away. But most of my life I was always taught sexual intimacy was only used for reproduction. Is this true? Signed: Enjoying the Fruit Before the Labor

A: Dear Enjoying the Fruit Before the Labor,

If you have agreed to live in a Christian home according to Christian principles, your authority is God and the Holy Scriptures. But understand first that any relationship where the two individuals are unequally yoked will be challenging. How can two walk together unless they agree? You did not mention if you accepted your fiancé's religion, you just indicated you accepted his proposal.

Intimacy is brought about by closeness and spending time with one another. Sexuality is one of the ways married couples express their intimacy. Yes, sex is for reproduction but it is also for fun. Sex is designed for procreation, recreation, stimulation, and much more. It is important for the two of you to agree to live according to the Bible, if you have accepted the faith of your future husband. Abstain from sex before marriage, enjoy one another sexually once you are married, and then be fruitful and multiply. Be open to God's timing for your family planning. It is a privilege to be entrusted with children and to raise godly seed. I recommend you and your fiancé seek premarital counseling to address the top four issues that trouble most couples (sex, children, communication, and finances). There may be habits and beliefs you need to address as you begin your marriage.

Q: I am 30 years old and was married for the first time when I was 18 (clearly we were both too young to get married). Now, years later, I've found my soul mate. My ex-husband and I have a pleasant relationship and did not have any children. Since I've found my new love and soul mate my question to you is concerning the biblical definition of adultery found in Mark 10:11–12: "He said to them, 'Whoever divorces his wife and marries another commits adultery against her; and if she divorces her husband and marries another, she commits adultery'" (ESV). And Romans 7:3, which says "She will be called an adulteress if she lives with another man while her husband is alive. But if her husband dies, she is free from that law, and if she marries another man, she is not an adulteress" (ESV). Was it wrong for us to admit we were both too young to get married and subsequently divorced? Now since I'm engaged to another, will this be considered adultery? Signed: Mrs. Right with Christ

A: Dear Mrs. Right with Christ,

If you were right with Christ, you would not be writing and asking these questions. Whenever we experience a dilemma or crisis of conscience, we question the decisions being made or the course we have chosen. Was it wrong for you to admit you were too young to get married? Of course not. You made a wise decision. Acknowledging your errors is the first step toward correcting it. However, sometimes the choices we make to correct problems create more problems—such as in your case. Getting divorced was not your only choice.

What issues led to your divorce? If it is years later, then you both should have matured by this point and worked through the issues of youth. Did you? What are you carrying into this next relationship? Is it considered adultery for you to marry again? Will that matter in your decision to proceed with the relationship? Did you seek counsel before your divorce? Seek counsel before you go further in this relationship. It sounds as if you still need to study the Scriptures and seek the face of God so you can make choices with a clear conscience.

God's law for marriage is a lifelong relationship between one man and one woman. When we break God's law, we are in sin. Your sin was divorce—thus the guilty conscience. Adultery is a sin and should be repented of just as with any other sins. John 1:9 says, "If we confess our sins, he is faithful and just to forgive us our sins, and to cleanse us from all unrighteousness" (KJV). Remember the woman that was caught in the very act of adultery in John 8:4–11? Follow the steps given above before you consider remarrying; repent, and then go and sin no more.

Q: My husband of thirty years is always on the Internet and has moved to the second bedroom. Each time I ask him if there is something he needs to tell me, he says I am his soul mate and I should not worry about this small bump in our relationship. How can I ask him to seek help, move back into the bedroom, and get off the Internet, without starting a war? Signed: Is This for Better or Worse?

A: Dear Is This for Better or Worse?

You are already in a battle to save your marriage. You just need to decide if you are going to stay in a cold war with no end and no victory, or would you rather have a heated war that could possibly end with a resounding victory? At any rate, the war will have an end. This is not the time to go along to get along. You both have a lot invested in your marriage, and as his soul mate you know this is more than a little bump in your relationship. This is like a pothole that will keep getting bigger until it wrecks your marriage.

Things like this usually get worse before they get better, and they don't get better by being left alone. You need to confront your husband in love and let him know this is destroying your life together. Things also don't get better in the dark or in isolation; this needs to be exposed to the light so others can help intervene. Talk with your husband about getting Christian counseling for your marriage. Don't just focus on his issues. Yes, he does need help, but you both need to be in full armor and equipped to fight the battle, not each other. The war is not against flesh and blood but against principalities and spiritual wickedness. The Lord can teach your hands to war so you can tear down strongholds in your marriage.

LET US PRAY

Lord, it is wonderful to acknowledge that I am a sexual being, without feeling any shame, and that is because I am your creation. Lord, thank you that I am fearfully and wonderfully made and that I am made in your image. I thank you, Lord, that you designed and assigned me my sexual gender. Lord, let me accomplish my purpose in your kingdom. Father, I thank you for the love of family and friends. Lord, prepare me for marriage and teach me how to guard and protect my sexuality. I pray that you will help me to regard my sexuality as a gift from you, to be unwrapped only after marriage. You said in your Word that we should all keep our bodies pure, that we should avoid sexual sin and remain celibate until marriage. Father, forgive me for times that I have made choices that were not pleasing to you. God, forgive me for the times when I did not remember my body was your temple. Break any unholy alliances or ties that I have made with my body. Help me to honor you and my body at all times. God, I thank you for being so loving and forgiving.

Scripture Truth to Help You LIVE RIGHT NOW

Category: SEX AND SEXUALITY

Now concerning the matters about which you wrote: "It is good for a man not to have sexual relations with a woman." But because of the temptation to sexual immorality, each man should have his own wife and each woman her own husband. The husband should give to his wife her conjugal rights, and likewise the wife to her husband. For the wife does not have authority over her own body, but the husband does. Likewise the husband does not have authority over his own body, but the wife does. Do not deprive one another, except perhaps by agreement for a limited time, that you may devote yourselves to prayer; but then come together again, so that Satan may not tempt you because of your lack of self-control.

1 Corinthians 7:1–5 (ESV)

I adjure you, O daughters of Jerusalem, by the gazelles or the does of the field, that you not stir up or awaken love until it pleases.

Song of Solomon 2:7 (ESV)

Because of this, God gave them over to shameful lusts. Even their women exchanged natural sexual relations for unnatural ones. In the same way the men also abandoned natural relations with women and were inflamed with lust for one another. Men committed shameful acts with other men, and received in themselves the due penalty for their error. Furthermore, just as they did not think it worthwhile to retain the knowledge of God, so God gave them over to a depraved mind, so that they do what ought not to be done. They have become filled with every kind of wickedness, evil, greed and depravity. They are full of envy, murder, strife, deceit and malice. They are gossips, slanderers, God-haters, insolent, arrogant and boastful; they invent ways of doing evil; they disobey their parents; they have no understanding, no fidelity, no love, and no mercy. Although they know God's righteous decree that those who do such things deserve death, they not only continue to do these very things but also approve of those who practice them.

Romans 1:26–32 (NIV)

"Food is meant for the stomach and the stomach for food"—and God will destroy both one and the other. The body is not meant for sexual immorality, but for the Lord, and the Lord for the body. And God raised the Lord and will also raise us up by his power. Do you not know that your bodies are members of Christ? Shall I then take the members of Christ and make them members of a prostitute? Never! Or do you not know that he who is joined to a prostitute becomes one body with her? For, as it is written, "The two will become one flesh." But he who is joined to the Lord becomes one spirit with him. Flee from sexual immorality. Every other sin a person commits is outside the body, but the sexually immoral person sins against his own body. Or do you not know that your body is a temple of the Holy Spirit within you, whom you have from God? You are not your own, for you were bought with a price. So glorify God in your body.

1 Corinthians 6:13–20 (ESV)

But I say, walk by the Spirit, and you will not gratify the desires of the flesh. For the desires of the flesh are against the Spirit, and the desires of the Spirit are against the flesh, for these are opposed to each other, to keep you from doing the things you want to do. But if you are led by the Spirit, you are not under the law. Now the works of the flesh are evident: sexual immorality, impurity, sensuality, idolatry, sorcery, enmity, strife, jealousy, fits of anger, rivalries, dissensions, divisions, envy, drunkenness, orgies, and things like these. I warn you, as I warned you before, that those who do such things will not inherit the kingdom of God.

Galatians 5:16–21 (ESV)

They have become callous and have given themselves up to sensuality, greedy to practice every kind of impurity. But that is not the way you learned Christ!—assuming that you have heard about him and were taught in him, as the truth is in Jesus, to put off your old self, which belongs to your former manner of life and is corrupt through deceitful desires, and to be renewed in the spirit of your minds, and to put on the new self, created after the likeness of God in true righteousness and holiness.

Ephesians 4:19–24 (ESV)

But sexual immorality and all impurity or covetousness must not even be named among you, as is proper among saints. Let there be no filthiness nor foolish talk nor crude joking, which are out of place, but instead let there be thanksgiving. For you may be sure of this, that everyone who is sexually immoral or impure, or who is covetous (that is, an idolater), has no inheritance in the kingdom of Christ and God.

Ephesians 5:3–5 (ESV)

For this is the will of God, your sanctification: that you abstain from sexual immorality; that each one of you know how to control his own body in holiness and honor, not in the passion of lust like the Gentiles who do not know God; that no one transgress and wrong his brother in this matter, because the Lord is an avenger in all these things, as we told you beforehand and solemnly warned you. For God has not called us for impurity, but in holiness. Therefore whoever disregards this, disregards not man but God, who gives his Holy Spirit to you.

1 Thessalonians 4:3–8 (ESV)

Let marriage be held in honor among all, and let the marriage bed be undefiled, for God will judge the sexually immoral and adulterous.

Hebrews 13:4 (ESV)

Live the Word. Live Right Now Application

Select five verses about sex and sexuality from the previous pages and complete these exercises.

Verse # 1 _____

How would you summarize this verse of Scripture?

_____

_____

_____

_____

What does the Bible verse mean to you? _____

_____

_____

Does this verse give you instructions for hope, help, or healing?

_____

As you read this verse of Scripture, do you feel the need to repent, reflect, or rejoice? _____

What do you need to do differently to live right now?

_____

_____

Name at least one person to whom you can be accountable and share your decision to live right now.

_____

Name at least one person you can encourage by sharing this Scripture. _____

Verse # 2 _____

How would you summarize this verse of Scripture?

_____

_____

_____

What does the Bible verse mean to you? _____

_____

_____

Does this verse give you instructions for hope, help, or healing?

_____

As you read this verse of Scripture, do you feel the need to repent, reflect, or rejoice? _____

What do you need to do differently to live right now?

_____

_____

Name at least one person to whom you can be accountable and share your decision to live right now.

_____

Name at least one person you can encourage by sharing this Scripture. _____

Verse # 3 _____

How would you summarize this verse of Scripture?

_____

_____

_____

What does the Bible verse mean to you? _____

_____

_____

Does this verse give you instructions for hope, help, or healing?

_____

As you read this verse of Scripture, do you feel the need to repent, reflect, or rejoice? _____

What do you need to do differently to live right now?

_____

_____

Name at least one person to whom you can be accountable and share your decision to live right now.

_____

Name at least one person you can encourage by sharing this Scripture. _____

Verse # 4 _____

How would you summarize this verse of Scripture?

_____

_____

_____

_____

What does the Bible verse mean to you? _____

_____

_____

Does this verse give you instructions for hope, help, or healing?

_____

As you read this verse of Scripture, do you feel the need to repent, reflect, or rejoice? _____

What do you need to do differently to live right now?

_____

_____

Name at least one person to whom you can be accountable and share your decision to live right now.

_____

Name at least one person you can encourage by sharing this Scripture. _____

Verse # 5 _____

How would you summarize this verse of Scripture?

_____

_____

_____

What does the Bible verse mean to you? _____

_____

_____

Does this verse give you instructions for hope, help, or healing?

_____

As you read this verse of Scripture, do you feel the need to repent, reflect, or rejoice? _____

What do you need to do differently to live right now?

_____

_____

Name at least one person to whom you can be accountable and share your decision to live right now.

_____

Name at least one person you can encourage by sharing this Scripture.

_____

CHAPTER 5

PARENTING

It's not only children who grow. Parents do too. As much as we watch to see what our children do with their lives, they are watching to see what we do with ours.

Joyce Maynard

And these words which I command you today, shall be in your heart. You shall teach them diligently to your children, and shall talk of them when you sit in your house, when you walk by the way, when you lie down, and when you rise up.

Deuteronomy 6:6–7 (NKJV)

Parenting has always had its share of joys and sorrows from the beginning of time. Since Adam and Eve, parents have needed God to walk with them and talk with them to help them raise a godly seed to populate the earth. Every step of the way, parents are in need of help via instructions and guidance. There were few books or classes on parenting when my parents or grandparents were raising children. The Bible served as their child-rearing guide, and with God's help, they raised a happy family. When I was growing up, parenting primarily meant one father and one mother with as many children as the Lord blessed them to have and nurture. A full quiver was a great joy. Every child was considered valuable because he or she was precious and given by God.

People did not marry, divorce, remarry, divorce, and remarry with the frequency of a revolving door. Couples did not have children outside of wedlock (intentionally) and those who did were the exception, not the norm. Getting married was an honorable estate that required total commitment "till death do you part," and one of the primary functions of marriage was sex and reproduction.

Parenting then and even still is an incredible responsibility that God has entrusted to adults. Parents are to teach and train their children to be good citizens on the earth, and to become prepared for citizenship in heaven. Parenting is at the core of our lives and it is the basic building block of our society. The way we raise our children or neglect to do so as parents affects all of us in some way.

Parenting is the primary responsibility of the father and mother. When I was a child others helped parent as well: older siblings, aunts, uncles, grandparents, and those "pretend" relatives in the neighborhood that had a sense of community and cared for children like they were their own. These carefully selected and sometimes self-appointed (yet approved) "others" were like a second set of parents to me; they would feed me, dress me in their child's clothing if needed, tell my parents on me, scold me, reprimand me, and buy me gifts for birthdays and Christmas.

Too many modern parents relegate their roles to the wrong "others." Now much of the rearing of our children has been relegated to the television, the Internet, school peers, and the government. The TV reinforces the mixed messages of society that are often anti-Christ, the Internet exposes them to a lost world without guidance, school teaches them the world's moral values and the world's view, and the government tells us how to discipline them. As a result of these trends, our children are missing the biblical view on moral teaching and training in the godly discipline they need to be good and productive citizens.

Parents need answers as they raise the next generation of world changers and leaders.

Parents need answers as they raise the next generation of world changers and leaders. They ask how to juggle home, careers, church, and then manage personal stress. They are searching for ways to help them understand how children are influenced and how to respond to what happens around them; how to establish and maintain reasonable limits; how to express love, affection, and compassion; how to motivate and teach their children about themselves; and how to be an advocate for them.

This chapter addresses parenting from the perspective of the Word. Each of the answers highlights a key area of Scripture: teaching a biblical view of life (Psalm 78:5–6; Deuteronomy 4:10; Ephesians 6:4), training and helping children develop skills and discover their strengths (Proverbs 22:6), and disciplining by teaching them the fear of the Lord and drawing the line consistently, lovingly, and firmly (Ephesians 6:1–4; Hebrews 12:5–11; Proverbs 19:18; Proverbs 29:15, 17).

Your children belong to you; act like it! Take responsibility for them. If you as parents are finding it difficult to navigate the waters of their childhood and to steer them successfully into adulthood, imagine how much more confusing it is for them. Children do a bad job of raising themselves and miss out on the natural impartation of knowledge and wisdom that parents provide.

For those of you who have raised children, are still nurturing them, or have watched others, you know that parenting is work and a full-time job. No matter how old, from toddler to teen and into adulthood, your children will always be your children. However, as they mature the dynamics of the relationship will and should change.

As you read through this section, think about how you would have handled the various real-life situations that parents are facing. Does your approach include teaching, training, and discipline from the world or the Word of God? What would you advise these parents and how would their lives change as a result?

- From Toddlers to Teens
- Adult Children
- Empty Nest
- Adoption/Foster Care
- Infertility
- Blended Families
- Grandparenting

Q: When will I be able to get some rest? From sun up to sun down I am taking care of the needs of my family:

cooking, cleaning, driving—you know the never-ending drill. Just because I am not working a nine-to-five my parents and sister are always making demands on my time too. I am so tired. My husband thinks that I sit in the house all day watching the stories and sitcoms on television. My children have no idea how much work I do around here and they are so ungrateful. It would be nice to be appreciated sometimes and to have my family realize that I would like to have a life. I really need just a little bit of time for myself and some rest. I hate to complain, but something has to change. Where do I start? Signed: I Need a Change

A: Dear I Need a Change,

Start with you! Take a deep breath right now, relax, and rest! Take ten minutes just for yourself. The Bible tells us to love others as we love ourselves. Don't wait for permission from others to rest and appreciate yourself. Go ahead and live your life; you may find your family more willing and happy for you to do so than you expected.

Be encouraged you are not alone. Most women and mothers will agree, to be a mom, a wife, and to have a life in this twenty-first century, you are going to have to be resilient like a rubber band. You must stretch and relax. If you don't, you will break or pop, which will hurt you and impact others. When you are stretched too much and have not had sufficient time to pull yourself back together, those around you know it. Reducing the stress in your life is in everyone's best interest. Read the stress strategies below and be ready to use them immediately.

Five Common Ways to Reduce Stress

- Read a book of quotes, prose, or poetry
- Listen to soft, soothing music
- Pamper yourself (rest, body massage, facial, manicure, makeover, etc.)
- Exercise (run, walk, bike, swim, play tennis, golf, garden, etc.)
- Make a list of ways to simplify your life

As you are looking at this list you may be thinking, "When and how will I do this?" You must make time for yourself. You cannot take care of your family if you are stressed out. Here are more things you can do that will help you reduce stress.

Spiritual Ways to Reduce Stress

- Encourage yourself with the Word of God and spiritual readings (C. S. Lewis, Max Lucado, Charles Spurgeon, etc.)
- Listen to songs of praise and worship
- Spend time in prayer and meditation
- Have fun and laugh out loud ("a merry heart doeth good like a medicine"—Proverbs 17:22)
- Give, share, or help someone else
- Pray without ceasing
- Praise God for who He is
- Remind yourself of what the Word says about peace
- Enjoy the life that God has given you

Be encouraged. Those who feel stretched can regain their resiliency and a renewed capacity. These simple strategies will help you in that process. You should already be feeling some relief as you have reviewed the ideas above. These essentials for beating stress and avoiding burnout are ideas you can implement today.

Yes, you do need a change but it also sounds like your household needs a change as well. Let them know that you are ready to draw a few loving lines and limits on what you will be doing. Give each of them chores and other tasks to do. Post the list of responsibilities in several highly visible areas of the house so that everyone can help monitor the workload and ensure things are completed. As you prepare to make these changes, read and meditate on these Scriptures:

- The LORD is a refuge for the oppressed, a stronghold in times of trouble. Psalm 9:9 (NIV)

- Cast your burden upon the LORD, and He will sustain you; He will never allow the righteous to be shaken. Psalm 55:22

- Don't worry about anything, but pray about everything. With thankful hearts offer up your prayers and requests to God. Philippians 4:6 (CEV)

- Cast all your anxiety on him, because he cares for you. 1 Peter 5:7 (NIV)

Q: I know that we were good parents to our children. Yet my three sons never call home unless they need something or we are preparing for the holiday. My husband doesn't think this is a problem, but my feelings are hurt. I gave and sacrificed so much for them. It seems the least they could do is call me. They are not bad boys; I just miss them so much. One is married with a new baby, and the other two are in college (freshman and senior years). Am I wrong? Am I expecting too much from them? Signed: Waiting by the Phone

A: Dear Waiting by the Phone,

Given today's technology, you can do more than wait by the phone. You can call, e-mail, text, Skype, Facebook, and more. Parents often send children away with prepaid credit cards or phone cards so they can stay somewhat connected (if needed). If you really wanted to, you could still hear their voice and see their smiling face every day. Don't make demands on your children to call you every night before bedtime. Let them grow up and go on with their lives as you do the same. You will grow together into a new relationship.

Are you expecting too much? Depends on who you ask. It is natural for a mother to want to stay connected with her children, but it is also natural to let them become adults and initiate a different type of relationship. These boys may have busy, active lives, with new friends and interests. It is not that you are less important but that you have raised them to be independent and they are making choices.

Before children go away to school, the house is home. When they are visiting on holiday most parents make it very clear, "this is my house and my rules." Yes, this is true, but don't be dogmatic. Your sons have been living on their own, setting their own rules and curfews. Their eating, sleeping, and hygiene habits may have even changed slightly. Don't automatically view their discovery of newfound freedom as rebellion. You will need to discuss and negotiate what is permissible when they visit. Don't make things so stringent that they can't wait to leave.

Q: I am so tired of my mother-in-law trying to make me fit into her vision of a homemaker. I have been doing all I could to keep peace in our family. My problems started when I was pregnant with our first child. I was having tea with my mother-in-law and she said, "You should think about quitting that job soon and start making a proper home now that you are expecting a baby, and a woman's place is in the home anyway." I was stunned to hear her say that. Since I was speechless, she went on to say that she was surprised Johnny had not made me quit that job when we first got married. I have a master's degree in science technology and I have a good job with prospects of promotion. Now whenever the family gets together she always wants to talk about me leaving that job. Why should I have to choose between a family and a career? My mother-in-law is not a mean person at all; she just has outdated views on life. She loves me and really thinks she is being helpful. We had a good relationship until I got pregnant and began to hear what she thinks. What can I say to her? I don't want to hurt her feelings. Signed: Stunned

A: Dear Stunned,

Staying home and being a housewife can be very satisfying; so can having a career in addition to your family. Let your mother-in-law know you appreciate her concern and words of wisdom. It is important that the lines of communication between you and your mother-in-law remain open for all involved. What you say will determine the direction of your relationship. Perhaps you can have this conversation over a meal with only the two of you present. In this manner your mother-in-law may be willing to put her opinion aside and give you a chance to share what you and your husband believe is best for you and your family.

It is certainly understandable that you would be taken aback by your mother-in-law's unwelcome advice. You and your husband should make the decision as to whether you work outside the home. Perhaps you should discuss your concerns with your husband so that he may address the issue with your mother-in-law. There are many schools of thought on whether a wife and mother should be a homemaker or a "career woman." However, each married couple must determine what is best for their household. Your mother-in-law may not realize how this is affecting you and a simple "thank you for your input" may suffice to quiet her comments. If she persists, then a more involved conversation may be necessary with your husband.

He can then explain to your mother-in-law that she has no right to enforce or dictate to you what should occur in your marriage. The function of your family should be determined by you and your husband, and your decisions should be respected. Point out to her that you obtained a degree for the purpose of pursuing a career and it would mean a lot to you if she would honor your decision. If your mother-in-law continues to bring up what role you should play in your marriage, you should refrain from a discussion that could escalate to feelings of anger or discontent. Be firm with your decision without verbalizing it repeatedly. I am sure your mother-in-law means no harm but is also just as firm about what she believes. Your mother-in-law may not change her mind about this matter. If she doesn't, simply leave the room whenever she brings it up, or change the subject using words of endearment by explaining that you love her and know she means well but your decision has been made and will stand. You could also suggest to your mother-in-law that you are going to give your career a chance and if necessary you are willing to take her advice into consideration.

Q: When I was young, children were told to "stay out of grown folks' business." You were not even to be in the room when adults gathered unless there were other children there. When the adults were talking, the young folks were supposed to be in another area of the house. This room was always out of listening and viewing range. I have raised my children the same way and so have most of my family members.

At a recent gathering at the home of a friend, her 7-year-old princess sat in the room among all of the adults. This was very uncomfortable for me and especially my husband, who is not strong in his faith. He already feels that my friends are watching him and waiting for him to say or do the wrong thing. As we went home, I had to hear about how he could not be himself because there was a child in the room watching his every move and interrupting the conversation. I'm not sure who I should be angry with and to whom I should address with my concerns: my husband or my friend? Signed: In the Middle of Grown Folks

A: Dear In the Middle of Grown Folks,

It is important that we are careful when offering childrearing advice to other, especially if it is a subject that is open for interpretation. I too grew up in the same era but have learned that like the book of Ecclesiastes advises in the Bible, the "good old days" may not quite be as good as we remember them. Every generation has its own challenges. Remember, you were a visitor in your friend's home. How would you feel if someone visited your home and began to criticize you for how you cleaned your home because it was different than how you were taught by their parents? Your issue seems to be more with the reaction of your husband than with your friend's childrearing practices. If you have an issue with the way in which your husband expressed his dislike for the presence of the child, you should discuss it with him. Suggest to him that you too found the child's presence unwelcome, but that you realized this was your friend's home and you had to adjust accordingly. Emphasizing, tactfully, to your husband the importance of allowing others to run their homes the way they see fit would likely be of more value than casting blame, which would only serve to do more harm than good. If he still feels uncomfortable after your talk, perhaps you should refrain from inviting him when you go to your friend's home. We cannot dictate and control what others allow in their home.

Q: I am a very happy homemaker; I love my husband and he loves me. Our children are our pride and joy. My husband has a good job and he is fine with me staying home to care for our family. He makes a good salary and takes good care of us. It is my family and friends, however, who are convinced that I cannot really be happy and that my husband is keeping me from living what they believe would be a fulfilling life. My friends are always leaving magazines or newspaper clippings about happy career women. I have a good education and could have a career, but I don't believe anything could make me happier than being with my children and having time to be engaged with them. I want to be present for that first smile, first word, and first step. Why can't they let me be happy as I am? Signed: Happy Homemaker

A: Dear Happy Homemaker,

Explain to your family and friends that while you know they mean well and you do appreciate them trying to be helpful, the decision you have made to be a homemaker should be respected. It is a decision you and your husband have made and it brings you great joy. There is untold value in being there for your children and engaging in their lives. Praise God for a husband who makes enough to financially allow you to stay home. He can care for you as you care for him and the children.

Q: We have been trying to have children for two years. When my husband and I were dating, he would talk endlessly about the children he hoped we would have. He was an only child and hoped to have a large family. Now, it seems I will not be able to give that to him. We have been going to fertility doctors but I just can't get my mind wrapped around having children through some type of science magic. I would like to bear my own children and feel them kick in my stomach. Why me? I have been a good person. I see my friends with their children and all I can think is, what did I do wrong? Signed: Wrong Turn

A: Dear Wrong Turn,

Be thankful that God has given such wisdom to those who have developed ways to help couples such as yourselves. You may yet feel that little one kicking, if not in you, then on you. What you are calling science magic is really a miracle from God! We don't know why some women do not give birth to children, but I can assure you that it is not because they are being punished because they did something wrong or took a wrong turn. The fertility doctors can work wonders with the help of God, but if it does not work, your husband's desire for children can still become a reality. There are other options for the two of you to explore. There are many children wanting and needing a good mother and a loving father; maybe this is God's plan for the two of you. Always remember you can be a child's mother without actually giving natural birth. Make the right turn, which is toward God. Seek His face, listen for His voice, and accept His plan for your life.

Q: I am 72 and my granddaughter is 15. How can I share the God of today with her when she is My Spacing, video watching, iPod listening, and the youth ministry in our church is billiards and board games? I have so much I want to share with her but I don't want to text to get her attention. Signed: Non-Tech Grandma

A: Dear Non-Tech Grandma,

Praise God for the seasoned saints that still desire to help young people "remember now thy Creator in the days of thy youth" (Ecclesiastes 12:1 KJV). We know that God is the same yesterday, today, and forever. The Lord is the Ancient of Days and the mercy of His presence is new every morning. God has always been relational and desired intimacy with His people. He has created us in His image with the same longing for connection and relationship. Beyond the technology and the gadgets is still a young lady who needs someone to talk to about living a life of holiness and righteousness (which will probably sound old-fashioned to her). Engage in conversation by asking her to help you learn how to use the iPod; listen to some of her songs and ask about the artists; take an interest in what she is doing. If you have time, go online with her and check out her social media profiles. Then while she is teaching you what she knows, you can teach her what you know. Don't fake it—young people know when we are not sincere. Remember parents have not agreed with their children's activities since the beginning of time, but it is a mistake to abandon them to it just because we don't like it. Our young people still need our guidance and the best way to give it is to be involved in their lives at home and at play. Myspace (or other social media sites), videos, iPods, billiards, and board games are not evil in and of themselves, so don't object to them. Just get involved and guide her as she makes choices about them. Check out what the Bible has to say in the book of Deuteronomy about consistently sharing our faith with our children. Walk with her the way Jesus walked with the disciples. You will be surprised that as she has your undivided attention and you have hers, you can impart amazing wisdom and biblical principles.

Q: My husband and I have raised seven children. They have been little to no trouble at all. We can truly say they have been a blessing from the Lord. The last one has gone away to college and I am at a lost on what to do with myself. We spent our days doing homework and meeting with teachers. When we were not at home, I was dropping someone off or picking someone up from band, cheerleading, or football practice. There was always laughter and joy as the children buzzed around the house.

My husband is excited that the children are all gone; he is looking at remodeling the house. He has taken up golf and is spending time at the gym. The ranges of emotions I feel go from anger toward him that he doesn't seem to miss them as much as I do to sadness and depression or loneliness and emptiness. I know it is natural for a mother to cry and feel some sadness when her children leave home, but I can't get over these feelings. My life seems to have no purpose now. With the children gone, what should I do? Signed: Full Quiver Now Empty

A: Dear Full Quiver Now Empty,

Yes, it is normal to have a little cry now and again as you remember the time when your house was filled with noise and laughter. Yes, it is sad to see them go away and leave home. But it can also be a time of celebration. Many people experience loss and grief when their children leave; you are not alone. As an empty nester, you may have lost those scheduled everyday routines that gave purpose and meaning to your life. Be encouraged. I am going to give you a different perspective or frame of reference when you think about having an empty nest.

All right, you have had a good cry; go wash your face and blow your nose. Make us (I mean you) some coffee or tea, whichever you prefer; we are going to talk. You do have time to talk this morning, don't you? Sure you do. As you have already indicated, you have too much time on your hands these days. Did you get something warm to drink? Sip it slow and get ready for what I am about to say. This will take a little time.

Empty by definition (in the context of empty nest) means unoccupied or uninhabited. It has also been used to mean unburdened, removed, transferred, or meaningless. These definitions would all imply that having an empty nest (the time of life when children transition to school, work, or a place of their own) leads to loneliness, lack of purpose, and vacant spaces in your heart and home. Not so. Let me help you reframe your thinking and encourage you in this next season of life.

This time of transition when your children are away at school is the mark of a new season in your life. Enjoy; celebrate graduation, the completion of one phase and the beginning of another. Remember that life with your children is a journey. You have moved from diapers and dirty dishes to dates and deadlines and now to days devoted to other areas of focus. Life doesn't end with an empty nest; it's another beginning, time for another adventure! Thank God for all the time you have had together and the many accomplishments. Yes, raising children that are ready and able to leave the nest is a great accomplishment. This is not the time to drag around being sad and lonely. Think of the things you have not been able to do over the past few years and start enjoying what you like instead of what they need.

Ask yourself the popular question, "How do I look?" or consider your home and ask yourself, "What changes would I make if I were going to redesign?" Now that your son or daughter has gone away to school, do a makeover. Just as your young people, now young adults, are making decisions about the image they want to project in their new environment, so also you can begin to consider redecorating.

This is a good time to makeover the space your son or daughter occupied. That room does not stay theirs forever. It is still part of your house; spread out in it. Set up a den, library, or guestroom. No, you are not putting your child out. Children should be welcomed home. But they are coming to visit, not live there again. The thought of this may be traumatic for all of you. So breathe, and just do a little at a time. The goal is to reflect a space that meets the needs of this phase in your life.

There is a proud moment when you look at your baby going away to school. You remember their first word, first steps, and when they learned to color inside the lines. You recall dates, school projects, and hours of completing applications. The big day is here. Your baby is becoming an adult, and although you will always be the parent no matter how old your child becomes, the relationship will change.

At some point you need to let them grow up and become an adult. Your child should always show you honor, respect, and consideration. However, they may not always do what you think is best. As a parent, hopefully you have invested time in helping them develop critical thinking skills so that they can make wise decisions and life choices. Remember, they are becoming responsible adults. Prepare for your relationship to change.

Most of your time has been spent transporting your child from one rehearsal and practice to the next. Most young people have such an active itinerary that their parents spend more time as a chauffeur than anything else. Now that they have gone, you have more time in your schedule. Ecclesiastes 3:1 tells us that "to everything there is a season, and a time to every purpose under the heaven" (KJV). When your season of caring for your children ends, it is a great time to get involved in hobbies, your church, or community activities.

Look for others in your age group that may also be sending children away to school and start a support group or social club depending on your emotional state and the need. This is a wonderful time to reconnect with your old friends. Often when we are raising children we neglect our friendships because of lack of time. Some of them may have already gone through this stage of life already and can share helpful insights.

Having faith in God and prayer can be a great comfort to you. Understanding that your purpose as a parent was to raise children to be independent adults, capable of leaving home and establishing homes for themselves, and in turn possibly raising children that will leave home, can help you see that the empty nest is part of God's plan.

Your children may be grown and gone, but there are still children who need you! Become a volunteer and work with your church youth group; your involvement with energetic young people will satisfy your mothering heart. It will be rewarding to see how much they need and appreciate your interest in them.

Rekindle the relationship with your spouse. Communicate with your spouse and tell him or her how you are feeling. Your husband's newfound freedom can be an example to you. Enjoy the time with him instead of being angry that he has adjusted. He may have even felt sad and lonely for a while too and will appreciate having someone to share the emotions. This time can be an amazing time to renew the intimacy you once shared and concentrate on your relationship. There are times when spouses feel abandoned as one or the other is totally invested in raising the children. Let him know that even though he may have felt forsaken, he is not forgotten. Make plans to take a trip (if you are not broke after preparing your children for college). This is a great time to take a much-needed vacation with your spouse or a friend.

A word about you and your self-esteem. Now that the children no longer live with you and you are not needed by them 24/7, how do see yourself? Can you identify yourself as a unique person in your own right? If not, it's time to make some changes. It's time to rediscover your life and get back in touch with who you are. Build up your confidence and start planning to establish and enjoy the life you dreamed of living before you became a mom. Remember the basis of your personal worth is not in what others think of you, it is not in your possessions, nor your talents, it is not even in being a great mom, but it is in knowing who you are in God. You are God's beloved daughter!

If the thought of letting go seems tragic or traumatic for you, consider getting some help. Don't laugh; I'm serious. If you are having thoughts of being useless, feel your life is over, or you are crying excessively for more than two weeks, you may want to call a Christian counselor who can help you through this change of life. If you are withdrawing from family and friends, find that you have difficulty sleeping, or have a hard time enjoying this newfound freedom, let someone know. Don't suffer in silence. You could benefit from talking out loud and getting your feelings into perspective.

Be encouraged! You are blessed; you have passed the test. The children you have raised are on their own. You have done your part to prepare them for life. Now establish a plan to live a life of overflow. You will rejoice when you realize the old thoughts of "empty" have been cured.

Q: We are considering adopting a child. We have one child of our own, but I always wanted my daughter to have a sister because I was an only child. I have not been able to have another baby. At this point I would take whatever the Lord would allow, boy or girl. It was lonely for me as an only child, and I said I would never allow that to happen to any child of mine. I have tried all the fertility drugs to no avail. Which brings me to my point: I would like to adopt a girl age 5 or 6 because my daughter is 7 and that way she could be the big sister. I don't know if I should go with foster parenting or adoption. Could you tell me the quickest way to make my dream come true? Signed: Ready for a Little Sister Now

A: Dear Ready for a Little Sister Now,

Why do you want to adopt? It is a wonderful thing to open your heart and home to a child by becoming a foster or adoptive parent. It will be a life-changing experience for you and your daughter. Some need temporary foster homes and are eventually able to return to their birth families. Some children need permanent homes through adoption.

You did not indicate whether or not you had prayed about the matter and God's response. There are times when we can want the right things for the wrong reasons or do the wrong things for what seems to be the right reasons. You are very clear that this is what you want, but your intensity to have another child also seems to be driven by your own experiences as a child. You may want to spend more time exploring the impact being an only child had on you and why you want to ensure your daughter doesn't have to go through it.

Studies have shown that only children have extremes in their personality ranging from completely competent and independent to totally needy and insecure. They can be high achieving scholars with leadership tendencies, having spent much of their time interacting with adults. They learn to communicate more clearly and process information at a different level than their peers. On the other hand, they can also be overstressed because of expectations from parents, themselves, and others. The need to measure up to the ideal little man or little women can cause them to feel oppressed and depressed. Only children also sometimes have limited social skills since there is no one to interact with on a consistent basis. But then they also fit in everywhere since they are accustomed to adapting to various situations and interacting with children in a variety of settings. Being an only child does not have to be a bad thing. How you parent the child will have the greater long-term impact. Again I say: consider your motives.

Before you bring home a child, be sure that both of you are ready. Does your daughter really want a little sister? Is your daughter really ready to share you with someone else? She will no longer be the sole focus of your parenting attention. Be careful to not make your daughter live your dreams.

When I was younger, I wanted a little sister for years so that I would have someone to help wash the dishes. It was not until later that I wanted her for companionship and camaraderie. When I was younger, a little sister would have been like a live Barbie doll to dress up and comb her hair. When I was older, it was so that we could share ideas about fashion and style.

If your motives are pure and you have the capacity for another addition, then and only then should you begin the process. There are so many children in the world that need a loving environment. Are you really ready to deal with the emotional drama that may come with the child? The child may be angry and resentful; maybe she has been abused physically, sexually, or emotionally. The child you think you are helping by taking her out of the system temporarily may not be grateful and thankful because what was normal has now changed. Are you prepared to have constant visits to your home and investigations into your background, as well as questions about your decision making on a monthly basis? Foster care is a big investment of time, money, energy, resources, and emotion. Yes, it brings great joy—but at a high cost. The return on your investment brings great dividends that you may end up sharing with someone else when the child is placed somewhere else.

Adoption also has its share of pros and cons. But everything that is involved is worth it when you are walking in God's will and fulfilling His purpose for your life. Whatever your decision, the Bible admonishes us to raise up a child in the way they should go. What may sound like a burden is actually a great joy when you know that this dream is bigger than just you. Just make your decision prayerfully and carefully.

Q: I have been married for ten years. My husband and I planned our family while we were dating. We both wanted to get our education and get good paying jobs before we started having children. We wanted to be able to give our children the best. I have been trying to conceive for five years. Now after three conceptions and three miscarriages, I am ready to just give up. I am angry and bitter because I see young unmarried girls with babies they can't care for financially, emotionally, or physically. Yet here I am with my arms empty and my heart yearning for a baby. Now I am afraid to get pregnant; the doctor has said if I have another miscarriage that I will have to forget about carrying a baby to full term. Please help; what should I do? Signed: Barren, Broken, and Bitter

A: Dear Barren, Broken, and Bitter,

I am so sorry to hear of your multiple losses. During the first six years of my marriage we tried desperately to get pregnant. When I did there was great joy. But shortly into the pregnancy I miscarried the only child that has come through my body. I have experienced many of the emotions you are going through and feel deeply your pain. There are several things that need to be addressed in your situation. The first being your love for and trust in God. He is still in control of your life and has plans for you. I can imagine you must be heartbroken. Take time to grieve your losses and all that being pregnant and having children represented for you and your husband. It is the Lord who gives and takes away and still we bless the name of the Lord. God determines who will have children and for what purpose even when we don't understand. Instead of being angry about the young unmarried girls, come alongside them and help them financially, emotionally, and physically. You are in a position to be a great blessing by sharing your heart, wealth, and wisdom. There is no need to be afraid. Spend time in prayer. Remind yourself that God is the great physician. Praise Him for being with you as you have gone through these hard times. Draw closer to the Lord and ask Him to reveal His will for your life. When your body cannot carry a baby full term, adoption or foster care is always an option.

Q: I am in love, love, love, and I want to marry this man in the worst way. I do not think I could be happy without him in my life. He loves me too. There is just this one problem—our kids! My three and his two do not like each other. My boys tolerate my boyfriend, but his girls seem to really hate me. Whenever we mention marriage or becoming a family they throw temper tantrums. They sulk, don't talk, talk back, and give us a hard time. His girls are 12 and 15; my boys are 7, 9, and 14. Can you give me some insight on blending our families? Am I trying to do the impossible? Signed: One Plus One Equals One

A: Dear One Plus One Equals One,

Blended families are more the norm than the exception since so many singles have children from previous marriages and relationships. They are more of a norm now than ever, with 65 percent of remarriages including children from previous relationships. When families "blend," things rarely progress smoothly. Some children may resist the many changes they face, while parents may become frustrated or disappointed when the new family doesn't function like their previous family. This is not a sitcom like *The Brady Bunch*. Each week will not begin with music and singing. There is no super housekeeper, counselor, or referee to help with the challenges of blending a family.

If you are serious about getting married, tell your children together and let them interact. Tell them how you feel about each other and your plans. Ask for their help in planning for a bigger home instead of moving them into your house or his.

Changes to family structure require some adjustment time for everyone involved. With the right guidance and realistic expectations, most blended families are able to work out their growing pains and live together successfully. Open communication, positive attitudes, mutual respect, and plenty of love and patience all have an important place in creating a healthy blended family.

Having survived a painful divorce or separation and then having found a new loving relationship, the temptation can often be to rush into remarriage and a blended family without first laying solid foundations. Consider the roles and involvement of all parents, including ex-spouses. How will their interaction be impacted by this blending? By taking your time, you give everyone a chance to get used to each other and used to the idea of marriage.

Keep in mind that boys and girls are different. As parents, we have different rules and expectations for each one. When children are in transition, girls want encouragement and praise—not physical affection. Boys accept fathers first, and then mothers. Girls adjust slower than boys. Children under 10 adjust faster. Children ages 10–14 have the most difficult time adjusting. Remember they are also dealing with hormonal changes. Children 15 and older may not be accepting and will avoid family time.

All children have some basic needs. Children want to feel safe and secure. Children want to be able to count on parents and step-parents. Children of divorce have already felt the upset of having people they trust let them down and may not be eager to give a second chance to a new step-parent. They want to be loved, even if they initially seem distant. Children like to see and feel your affection, although it should be a gradual process. They want to be seen and valued. Kids often feel unimportant or invisible when it comes to decision making in a new blended family. Recognize their role in the family when you make decisions. Children also need loving limits even if they fight against them. Boundaries are good for all children and should be supported by both parents.

I know you love, love, love this man but the truth be told, you could live without him. Having him in your life may make things better and bring joy into your life, but at what cost to the children? They are your primary responsibility until they are 21. I pray that you love, love, love them just as much, and enough to really consider their feelings and their future.

LET US PRAY

Abba, Father, you are the ultimate parent! Thank you for being my father. You are loving, wise, understanding, forgiving, and kind. You are always right and just. You are all knowing, all seeing, and present everywhere! How great you are. I pray that you will fill me with your love, so I can love my children unconditionally. Help me to train them and teach them who you are so their hearts will be turned toward you. I thank you for the instructions you give in your Word. I pray that I will give my children the discipline and counsel they need to become godly citizens while they are here on earth, but more than that I want them to understand that they are training to become citizens of heaven. Lord, forgive me for times when I was not the best parent. Forgive me for any bad attitudes that I have had toward my own parents. If it is not too late, let me show them love and honor. I want to be a blessing to my mother and my father. Let me set a good example for my children to follow as I follow you. Thank you, Lord. In Jesus' name I pray, amen!

Scripture Truth to Help You LIVE RIGHT NOW

Category: PARENTING

You shall love the LORD your God with all your heart and with all your soul and with all your might. These words, which I am commanding you today, shall be on your heart. You shall teach them diligently to your sons and shall talk of them when you sit in your house and when you walk by the way and when you lie down and when you rise up.

Deuteronomy 6:5–7

He gives the barren woman a home, making her the joyous mother of children. Praise the LORD!

Psalm 113:9 (ESV)

Behold, children are a heritage from the LORD, the fruit of the womb a reward. Like arrows in the hand of a warrior are the children of one's youth. Blessed is the man who fills his quiver with them! He shall not be put to shame when he speaks with his enemies in the gate.

Psalm 127:3–5 (ESV)

My child, if sinners entice you, turn your back on them!

Proverbs 1:10 (NLT)

My son, obey your father's commands, and don't neglect your mother's instruction.

Proverbs 6:20 (NLT)

Only a fool despises a parent's discipline; whoever learns from correction is wise.

Proverbs 15:5 (NLT)

Train up a child in the way he should go; even when he is old he will not depart from it.

Proverbs 22:6 (ESV)

Do not hold back discipline from the child, although you strike him with the rod, he will not die.

Proverbs 23:13

Children, obey your parents because you belong to the Lord, for this is the right thing to do. "Honor your father and mother." This is the first commandment with a promise: If you honor your father and mother, "things will go well for you, and you will have a long life on the earth."

Ephesians 6:1–3 (NLT)

Likewise, you who are younger, be subject to the elders. Clothe yourselves, all of you, with humility toward one another, for "God opposes the proud but gives grace to the humble."

1 Peter 5:5 (ESV)

Live the Word. Live Right Now Application

Select five verses about parenting from the previous pages and complete these exercises.

Verse # 1 _____

How would you summarize this verse of Scripture?

_____

_____

What does the Bible verse mean to you? _____

_____

_____

Does this verse give you instructions for hope, help or healing?

_____

As you read this verse of Scripture, do you feel the need to repent, reflect, or rejoice? _____

What do you need to do differently to live right now?

_____

_____

Name at least one person to whom you can be accountable and share your decision to live right now.

_____

Name at least one person you can encourage by sharing this Scripture.

_____

Verse # 2 _____

How would you summarize this verse of Scripture?

_____

_____

What does the Bible verse mean to you? _____

_____

_____

Does this verse give you instructions for hope, help or healing?

_____

As you read this verse of Scripture, do you feel the need to repent, reflect, or rejoice? _____

What do you need to do differently to live right now?

_____

_____

Name at least one person to whom you can be accountable and share your decision to live right now.

_____

Name at least one person you can encourage by sharing this
Scripture. _____

Verse # 3 _____

How would you summarize this verse of Scripture?

_____

_____

_____

What does the Bible verse mean to you? _____

_____

_____

Does this verse give you instructions for hope, help or healing?

_____

As you read this verse of Scripture, do you feel the need to
repent, reflect, or rejoice? _____

What do you need to do differently to live right now?

_____

_____

Name at least one person to whom you can be accountable and share your decision to live right now.

_____

Name at least one person you can encourage by sharing this Scripture. _____

Verse # 4 _____

How would you summarize this verse of Scripture?

_____

_____

_____

What does the Bible verse mean to you? _____

_____

_____

Does this verse give you instructions for hope, help or healing?

_____

As you read this verse of Scripture, do you feel the need to repent, reflect, or rejoice? _____

What do you need to do differently to live right now?

_____

_____

Name at least one person to whom you can be accountable
and share your decision to live right now.

_____

Name at least one person you can encourage by sharing this
Scripture. _____

Verse # 5 _____

How would you summarize this verse of Scripture?

_____

_____

_____

What does the Bible verse mean to you? _____

_____

_____

_____

Does this verse give you instructions for hope, help or healing?

_____

As you read this verse of Scripture, do you feel the need to repent, reflect, or rejoice? _____

What do you need to do differently to live right now?

_____

_____

Name at least one person to whom you can be accountable and share your decision to live right now.

_____

Name at least one person you can encourage by sharing this Scripture.

_____

CHAPTER 6

SELF-IMAGE

I have to live with myself, and so I want to be fit for myself to know.

Edgar Guest

But we all, with open face beholding as in a glass the glory of the Lord, are changed into the same image from glory to glory, even as by the Spirit of the Lord.

2 Corinthians 3:18 (KJV)

Our self-image is the way we see ourselves, and the reflection we see is not always true, especially when we are looking in the wrong mirror. However, once we have formed a concept of what and who we are, true or not, it is hard to change what we think we are. We are not born with a negative self-image; it is imposed on us by our surroundings and the attitudes of others toward us. The Word of the Lord can renew our minds and wash away the views of the world and the images we receive.

It is important for a child to read and to hear what God has to say about him or her. Receiving positive feedback about his or her character, work, and looks is also important. Knowing that you "are fearfully and wonderfully made" serves as a shield against all the darts thrown at you daily. When you know you are loved because God loves you, that you are capable because the Word says you can do all things through Christ who strengthens you, and that you are smart because you have the mind of Christ Jesus and your head is crowned with wisdom, the impact of the world's view is limited.

When you know that you have worth not just because of the gifts, talents, abilities, and skills that God has given, it will improve your self-image. We need to be mindful that man looks at the outward appearance but God looks at the heart (1 Samuel 16:7). As children are struggling with their weight, height, and other features, we need to show them how they look in a mirror that really matters, the mirror of the Word. My mother taught me early on that pretty is as pretty does, so I did not worry about my looks as much. I thought more about my actions because I knew they were the outcome of what was in my heart. I behaved beautifully so I would feel

> **God has uniquely formed and fashioned each of us.**

beautiful. If ever I stood in front of the glass mirror too long, even now as an adult, I could hear my mother reminding me of the words in Proverbs 31:30, "Charm is deceptive and beauty does not last; but a woman who fears the LORD will be greatly praised" (NLT).

Our self-image is based on how we see ourselves, how others see or act toward us, or how we believe others see us. The world either reinforces or refutes our self-image through commercial products and other media sources. I remember the first time I was hurt and confused because someone thought it was unusual for me to be pretty because I was black with long wavy hair! The world would say to those who are dark, "bleach your skin" and to those who are light, "get a tan." The world says to those who are short, "wear six-inch heels" and to those who are tall, "wear flats." The world wants us to camouflage what God has made and deemed beautiful in His sight. Most people initially remember my long hair (which is now streaked by God with silver strands) and the richness of my color complexion. They also remember my character. God took what others thought was strange to allow people to distinguish me from the crowd. It is ironic that the kid with the big feet that becomes a famous runner forgets that others used to tease him. God has uniquely formed and fashioned each of us. We are special in His sight.

> *We must not let those holding pre-formed opinions based on insufficient knowledge, irrational feelings, or inaccurate stereotypes determine how we see or feel about ourselves.*

The world may try to stereotype us and put us in a mold or stamp us out with its cookie cutter, or lump us all together as "too . . ." because of its prejudices. Just remember there has always been a plan for your life that includes the way God made you. Helping people young and old embrace their uniqueness improves their sense of worth and value; God made them the way they are on purpose. He formed and fashioned us based on His calling for our lives.

It is in our power and up to us to reclaim or retain the fact that we are created in the image of God and after His likeness. We must not let those holding pre-formed opinions based on insufficient knowledge, irrational feelings, or inaccurate stereotypes determine how we see or feel about ourselves.

In the beginning when God created the heavens and the earth, he had you in mind. We know from Genesis 1:27–28 that God created male and female, blessed them, and told them to be fruitful and multiply. However, if you read that Scripture slowly you will realize that even before God said be fruitful and multiply, He said "be . . ." We can be everything that the Lord planned for us to be. He did not say "try to be"; He just said, "Be." We are human beings, becoming what it has always been in us to be. Even when the world around did not understand who she was, Mary, the mother of our Lord, said these words in Luke 1:38, "Be it unto me according to thy word" (KJV). What is the Word of the Lord for you, for me, for us? We can be, because God is. All that the Great I Am says I am is so.

Neil Anderson in his book *Victory Over the Darkness* provides a great list of "I AMs" for the believer to live. When we embrace the truth of these words taken from Scripture, our sense of significance, value, and worth is increased. Our level of confidence, capacity, and security is established. Look at the list and say the words aloud so that you can hear the voice of the Lord louder than the voices in the world.

I AM a child of God (Romans 8:16)

I AM redeemed from the hand of the Enemy (Psalm 107:2)

I AM forgiven (Colossians 1:13, 14)

I AM saved by grace through faith (Ephesians 2:8)

I AM justified (Romans 5:1)

I AM sanctified (1 Corinthians 6:11)

I AM a new creature (2 Corinthians 5:17)

I AM delivered from the powers of darkness (Colossians 1:13)

I AM led by the Spirit of God (Romans 8:14)

I AM free from all bondage (John 8:36)

I AM kept in safety wherever I go (Psalm 91:11)

I AM strong in the Lord and in the power of His might (Ephesians 6:10)

I AM doing all things through Christ who strengthens me (Philippians 4:13)

I AM an heir of God and a joint heir with Jesus (Romans 8:17)

I AM heir to the blessings of Abraham (Galatians 3:13, 14)

I AM blessed coming in and blessed going out (Deuteronomy 28:6)

I AM an heir of eternal life (1 John 5:11, 12)

I AM blessed with all spiritual blessings (Ephesians 1:3)

I AM healed by His stripes (1 Peter 2:24)

I AM above only and not beneath (Deuteronomy 28:13)

I AM more than a conqueror (Romans 8:37)

I AM an overcomer by the blood of the Lamb and the word of my testimony (Revelation 12:11)

I AM walking by faith and not by sight (2 Corinthians 5:7)

I AM casting down vain imaginations (2 Corinthians 10:4–5)

I AM bringing every thought into captivity (2 Corinthians 10:5)

I AM being transformed by renewing my mind (Romans 12:1, 2)

I AM the righteousness of God in Christ (2 Corinthians 5:21)

I AM an imitator of Jesus (Ephesians 5:1)

I AM the light of the world (Matthew 5:14)

You are what God says you are and you can do what the Lord says you can do. There are no qualifiers to these powerful reminders. Parents, background, education—none of these affects the promises of God. When you are tired of pretending, performing, and pleasing, when you are ready to live right, the word of the Lord will quicken in your spirit and there will be great relief. These "I AM" statements are not based on you being like anyone else but you. They are not based on our performance but will influence it. They are not based on the applause of men, although men will marvel at the confidence you exude when you believe. I can hear the Word of the Lord and be who God says I am. When you believe God's Word, then you live God's Word. When you believe God's Word, you are free to be who you have always been and free to become who you are destined to be. When you believe God's Word, it gives you a boldness to step out in faith. Think of the number of decisions you have made, things you may have avoided attempting, or simply the opportunities you have missed because you were not clear of your identity in Christ. Embracing this truth will transform your thinking, your actions, and your life.

Q: It is so hard being the middle child. I know most people think it is all hype, but believe me it is no joke to try to live up to someone else's image. Yes, I am the middle daughter. My parents wonder where I came from and so do I. Because they remind me in so many little ways that I am not as pretty and popular as my older sister, and I am not as smart and loving as my baby sister. They imply that I should try to be more like my sisters. They make me feel different and like an outsider. Signed: The Middle Child

A: Dear Middle Child,

No one wants to hear about how good another person is, especially when that person's great characteristics and strengths are used to point out your shortcomings and to put you down. No one wants to feel that he or she does not measure up to their parents' expectations or that being like someone else would be better. Most of us know we are not perfect. We can all use some improvement. God isn't finished with us yet. However, we don't want our worth and values to be determined by our birth order, or how much we are or are not like someone else.

As individuals, we are usually guilty of too much self-analysis and personal reflection. We list our faults and weaknesses and know the things we need to change—things such as weight, hair color, clothing style, bad habits, and quirks. Yet, we still have desirable traits and characteristics. We want to be accepted by people who recognize and celebrate our good traits. You did not mention your age, but if you are still living with your parents, respect and honor them. You may need help dealing with your feelings. Talk with your parents about this.

Q: Please help me! I am 26 years old and I am so depressed. Life hardly seems worth living. I love God and I am faithful and dutiful at my church. But I don't see how God can love me because no matter how hard I try I cannot truly testify that I am perfect and free from sin as the leaders in my church do. I live in constant terror of going to hell. I need a godly man to pray for me as it is hard for me or any woman to come close enough to God to pray effectively. Maybe I will never be free from sin because I am a woman. We are by nature historically responsible in Mother Eve for the pollution of humankind in original sin. What can I do to please God as a woman? Signed: Can I Ever Be Worthy of His Love?

A: Dear Can I Ever Be Worthy of His Love?

When Jesus died on the cross for your sins, He already deemed you to be worthy and valuable. You did nothing to earn His love. God has already decided that you are lovable, forgivable, valuable, and changeable. His desire is that you would draw near to Him, love Him, and obey Him. In Jeremiah 31:3 the Lord tells us, "I have loved you with an everlasting love; I have drawn you with loving-kindness" (NIV). The Lord also declares in Isaiah 43:4, "Since you are precious in My sight, since you are honored and I love you, I will give other men in your place and other peoples in exchange for your life."

God does not love you because you are perfect; He is perfecting you because He loves you. It is the great relief of those who love the Lord and know His Word to realize that according to Philippians 1:6, "Being confident of this, that he who began a good work in you will carry it on to completion until the day of Christ Jesus" (NIV). God knows what He is doing in, through, and in spite of you; He loves you.

Unfortunately, you are living a life of desperation. It must be challenging for you to be depressed to the point where life does not seem worth living or to be in such despair and tormented with thoughts of hell. Christ has died that you might live and live life more abundantly. He has conquered hell and the grave that as you believe in Him, you might have eternal life.

Your freedom in Christ is not based on your gender. Your ability to pray and be heard by the God of heaven has nothing to do with your gender. In the kingdom of heaven, "There is neither Jew nor Greek, there is neither bond nor free, there is neither male nor female: for ye are all one in Christ Jesus" (Galatians 3:28 KJV). What you can do to please God is to be obedient to His Word. He tells us to not be conformed to this world but to "be transformed by the renewing of your mind, that ye may prove what is that good, and acceptable and perfect will of God" (Romans 12:2 KJV).

Stop thinking like the world and measuring yourself according to the outward appearance. Stop thinking that women are inferior and that you are being punished for the sin of Eve. God made you a woman and He did not make a mistake. Whoever suggested to you that a woman could not pray as effectively as a man? There is no hint in the Bible of such an idea.

God knows what is best for us; He who began a good work in you will finish it. Just stay on course, stay focused, and keep your eyes fixed on Jesus. The Lord will not forsake the works of His hands; He will perfect that which is concerning you (Psalm 138:8). The Lord has promised to pour out His Spirit on all flesh. Yield yourself for this great outpouring and walk worthy.

Q: I have become self-destructive. I am scared that one day I will go too far and kill myself. I don't want to die. I just feel this need to suffer for my sins. I was raised with very high moral standards and have fallen into such sin that I am useless to God. I do not feel worthy of the blood of Christ because of the way I disregarded His sacrifice through my lifestyle. I hoped to prove myself worthy of the grace of God through actually suffering and crucifying my own flesh. I tried to pay for the sins I have fallen into with my own blood. This led to behaviors such as cutting myself and binge eating, and then throwing up the food. I keep trying to discipline my body into following Christ. When I fail, I go back to even more destructive behaviors. Signed How Do I Break This Cycle of Self-Abuse?

A: Dear How Do I Break This Cycle of Self-Abuse?

"[You] shall not die, but live, and declare the works of the LORD." (Psalm 118:17 KJV). I am encouraged to read that you do not want to die. God does not want you to die before your time either; He wants you to live and for your life to bring Him glory. Just as God delivered David's soul from death and his eyes from tears and his feet from falling in Psalm 116:8, He can and will do the same thing for you.

Self-destructive behavior patterns, self-mutilation, and/ or self-injury (terms which may be used interchangeably) are primitive means for combating emotional numbness. These actions seek to replace emotional pain with a physical one, as if it will make life become more bearable. There are times when the inner anguish can seem so unbearable that you would rather feel outer pain. Self-destructive behavior patterns can also become a way that is easier to demonstrate that you are in pain when the injury is visible and physical rather than "just psychological."

Some of the behaviors you describe such as eating disorders and mutilation are among the most common forms of self-destruction. Other common forms are alcohol abuse, drug abuse, and gambling addiction. There are times when the destructive behavior is self-sabotage or self-defeating. These behaviors can cause you irreparable harm or damage, either deliberately or inadvertently. We need to repent of our sins, not pay penance for our sins. I do not know what you have done or what others have done to you, but repentance and forgiveness are the answer. God does not want you to feel guilty about your behavior, but to have godly sorrow that leads to repentance.

It sounds as if your theology may be slightly confused. When truth is mixed with fallacy we end up believing a lie upon which we base our decision. It is true that "without the shedding of blood there is no forgiveness" (Hebrews 9:22). However, the blood of Jesus has already been shed and paid for your sins; there is no need for you to shed blood. "For Christ died for sins once for all, the righteous for the unrighteous, to bring you to God. He was put to death in the body but made alive by the Spirit" (1 Peter 3:18 NIV). Jesus has made the necessary blood sacrifice for us. We can now enter into fellowship with God by believing and accepting this sacrifice for ourselves. So you see there is no need for you to bring a physical sacrifice; God is not delighting in that anymore.

The sacrifice God wants you to bring is a spirit of repentance. "You do not delight in sacrifice, or I would bring it; you do not take pleasure in burnt offerings. The sacrifices of God are a broken spirit; a broken and contrite heart, O God, you will not despise" (Psalm 51:16–17 NIV). In Hebrews 10:19–23 we read:

> Therefore, brothers, since we have confidence to enter the Most Holy Place by the blood of Jesus, by a new and living way opened for us through the curtain, that is, his body, and since we have a great priest over the house of God, let us draw near to God with a sincere heart in full assurance of faith, having our hearts sprinkled to cleanse us from a guilty conscience and having our bodies washed with pure water. Let us hold unswervingly to the hope we profess, for he who promised is faithful. (NIV)

This cycle of self-destruction can be broken with the truth of God's Word. A Christian counselor can walk alongside you to help unravel the deeply entrenched faulty belief system, replace the lies of the world with the truth of the Word, and show you how to apply it. You need to learn about the love of God so that you can learn to love yourself. You should also learn more about the forgiveness of God, for He is not holding your sins against you.

Call for help immediately and meditate on the following Scripture as you wait for your appointment: "To do what is right and just is more acceptable to the LORD than sacrifice" (Proverbs 21:3 NIV).

Q: Two weeks ago I received a promotion on my job. Most of my friends congratulated me with greeting cards. One of my co-workers gave me a business card to a professional image consultant. I want to believe it was well meaning especially since she paid the consulting fee, but still I wonder whether I really need an image consultant. Who I am and the way I am was obviously enough for me to get the job. Improving or enhancing my image was not mentioned on any of my recent performance evaluations. So I am baffled. I have already said thank you and I do plan to go. But how does a person know that this is needed? Signed: Promoted Yet Puzzled

A: Dear Promoted Yet Puzzled,

Do you need an image consultant? That is a good question. The list of positions that rely on image consultants might include politicians, corporate executives, television and movie actors, athletes, ministers, speakers, and mid-level executives such as you who want to be or have been promoted. The truth is that everyone who interacts with the public (you and I included) needs an image consultant. Image consulting is not just about glitz and glamour—it is going to the gut and dealing with the inside.

Image consulting is not just cleaning up or polishing the outside; it is cleaning up your character. Even as Christians we need an image consultant. We need to consult with the Holy Spirit to make sure we are bearing the image of Christ. We need to be washed in the Word of God. We need to have our minds renewed and our spirits refreshed. We need to know God and reflect to others that we know Him. Yes, an image consultant will help you look good, dress appropriately, and look the part. But remember, it is not just about looking better; it is about being better, being the you God created you to be. Your boss obviously saw past the exterior and hired a person of character. Enjoy the makeover and remind yourself when it is done that you already had the job, the new look is just extra.

Q: I hate the term "Army Wife." As much as I love my country, I am not married to the military and feel that I have sacrificed too much for the sake of the war. What do I do when I have given up all my dreams and desires to follow my husband and he goes nowhere? We are not experiencing the many benefits of his service. He proudly wears the badge of honor but to his dishonor we have very little. My husband has served three terms (he re-enlisted twice). Signed: When Is It My Turn?

A: Dear When Is It My Turn?

There is no point in hating something or someone you cannot change. You knew who he was when you married him. He is pursuing his dream. What about you? Are you experiencing the abundant life in Christ? Do you have a sense of purpose and direction? What is your kingdom dream? The term "Army Wife" has been around a long time and was never meant to indicate that you are married to the military, but that you are married to an honorable man who serves his country in the military. I don't know what you have sacrificed; you were not asked to make these sacrifices for the sake of war but for the sake of the country you love so much and to support the man you love. Whether they are in military families or not, wives will generally move with their husbands to be near their jobs, and still try to achieve their goals, even though it may be more challenging to do so. Your dissatisfaction seems to be more about your husband's lack of achievement and the absence of material things. To his credit he is proud to serve his country, and there is no dishonor in having little. You too should use your gifts to make a difference. Don't take your talents to the grave. Get involved in your church or community, begin to volunteer and discover the joy of serving as you follow your dreams. Even if you have children, it is still your turn to make a difference. Start with your family.

Q: My husband and I both lost over fifty pounds last year. Somehow though, I am the bigger loser even though he lost more weight. We changed our eating habits, exercised, and trained tougher. We both look great. He has always been handsome but now he thinks that he is too good for me. Those are not his words but his demeanor; his ego is larger than life. We both attract a lot of attention from others. I'm afraid he may begin to respond. Signed: Losing Him Now That the Weight Is Gone

A: Dear Losing Him Now That the Weight Is Gone,

Don't let your fear rob you of the victories you both have won. You have spent the last few months working on the same goal, now enjoy it. Since you both attract a lot of attention from others, are you sure he thinks that he is too good for you, or is it that you think you are not good enough for him because he is so handsome? You both have a right to feel proud of what you have achieved together. Give him the respect and admiration he needs. Congratulate him on what you accomplished together and he will be so busy responding to you that you will not have to fear his response to others.

Q: I'm 31 years old and have been in a long-term relationship for some time now. I have young children but my boyfriend has none. I'm so ready to get married, but my boyfriend has one excuse after another. I know that I need to leave him. How do I get the strength? Signed: Weak for Him and Tired of Waiting

A: Dear Weak for Him and Tired of Waiting,

Are you weak for him or just weak? How long have you been waiting? There comes a time when you need to draw the line in the sand. Long-term relationships can lead to major temptations. In some relationships we experience too much too soon; in others we become bored and want more and more. If it is really a long-term relationship, the two of you have had an opportunity to experience each other in many situations. You know each other's character, temperament, strengths, and weaknesses. He knows that you have become used to waiting and are willing to live with his excuses. If this is not the life you want for you and your children, then it is time to let him know something else about you. Be clear about your desires and expectations as well as his apparent relational limitations. Wake up and stand up, open the eyes of your understanding and realize that no matter how ready you are to get married, your friend is not ready, and it is only legal if you both say "I do." Your friend has a lifestyle that obviously satisfies him and he has not changed. You will need to make the change in your relationship by moving on with your life. Consider your children; as a mother you need to make good choices for yourself as well as for them. If he is not ready to marry, he also may not be ready to be a father. If your children's father(s) are involved in their lives, how does it affect your relationship with your long-term boyfriend? You said you know you need to leave him. Let me tell you a secret: it does not take strength to leave him; it takes action! Get moving and you will find you are strong enough to do it.

Q: I am about to complete my freshman year in college. I am away from my Christian home and am sharing the suite with two females I do not know and one that I have known since junior high school. I need to ask you about sharing my faith. The other two females are openly gay and in a relationship. I feel this is a violation of my rights as a roommate as well as a Christian. However, I am afraid to say anything because my other roommate said it would be considered bullying! What can I do because I feel like I am being bullied? Signed: Where Are My Rights?

A: Dear Where Are My Rights?

Your rights are hiding behind your fear. We all have the right to live where we are not violated, but we have no right to actions that violate the rights of others. Your two gay roommates are exercising their right to be together and will continue to do so until you exercise your rights as a Christian and a room-mate, and object to them violating a shared space. You do not want to be a bully, but you do want to stand up for what you believe, so share your beliefs in a respectful way and refuse to be bullied into denying your faith. This is an opportunity for you to witness. Pray before you approach them. Talking with your roommates in a non-threatening way would not be bullying. When you are living in an uncomfortable situation you should be able to say so. What is going on that makes you feel bullied? Are you being pressured to participate? Are they acting out in front of you? Are you being forced out of the room by the other ladies? What does the student hand-book say concerning student behavior in the rooms? There are usually guidelines regarding fraternizing and/or sexual activities in the room (the things that apply to the guys also apply to the girls). Is there a resident assistant you can talk with? If all this fails, consider transferring to another room.

Q: My life is a complete fake. Don't get me wrong, I have a very good job, house, and car. I am well-dressed and can recite the Scripture with the best of them. I usually have the best advice when it comes to problems. But I have no respect for others. I look down on everyone that doesn't have what I have or better. Some consider me very judgmental, I find fault all the time, and have little to no patience. Proverbs 12:15 always comes to mind but I cannot control myself. Signed: Smoke and Mirrors

A: Dear Smoke and Mirrors,

Praise God that although you may be fooling others, God is allowing you to see yourself. Usually when someone looks in the mirror and sees that his face is dirty, he begins to wash away the dirt and the filth. When God allows us to behold that we are like filthy rags, even those who believe they have it all together, He gives us room for confession and repentance. Go ahead and really ask God to wash away your pride. What do you have that God did not give you? Nothing. So what are you so uppity about? It is not the things in life that make you who you are; it is your character. Take the risk to allow people to really see you and get to know you. Many times when we find fault in others, the things we identify are a reflection of the very things we don't like in ourselves. You may want to list the areas that you seem to always criticize in others and ask God to reveal your weaknesses in these areas. It is not always easy to see our own imperfections. Consider praying Psalm 51:10–12, "Create in me a clean heart, O God; and renew a right spirit within me. Cast me not away from thy presence; and take not thy holy spirit from me. Restore unto me the joy of thy salvation; and uphold me with thy free spirit" (KJV). Take heed to your own Scripture reference in Proverbs 12:15, "The way of a fool is right in his own eyes: but he that hearkeneth unto counsel is wise" (KJV). And Proverbs 16:18: "Pride goes before destruction, and a haughty spirit before a fall" (ESV).

Q: I am a 19-year-old, attractive female. I am a high achiever. I have a smile on my face every day; no one knows that I cry myself to sleep almost every night. I help everyone around me, but really I need help myself. I am a substance abuser. I just need to use it in social situations. I wear revealing clothing to please people. I am so tired of faking it. Signed: How Can I Become a Real Person?

A: Dear How Can I Become a Real Person?

I'm so glad you asked. It is good that you realize you are achieving much. Let me remind you that the many abilities you have come from a God who loves you. Even before we become Christians, God has placed on the inside of us everything we need to become a real person. This deposit He has made is fully activated when we accept Christ and come into the fullness of what the Lord has for us. "For we are His workmanship, created in Christ Jesus for good works, which God prepared beforehand that we would walk in them" (Ephesians 2:10).

All those terms you and others have used to describe yourself—high achiever, substance abuser—are the things that are not real. They do not define you. Being a real person is about being who God has destined you to become. Galatians 2:20 can serve as a reminder for you: "I am crucified with Christ; nevertheless I live; yet not I, but Christ liveth in me: and the life which I now live in the flesh I live by faith in the Son of God" (KJV). It can be challenging to be real when we're going by the world's definition instead of God's definition. His criteria for "real" is so much easier to live up to.

As you spend time in the Word of God learning more about what He has to say about you, you will find yourself experiencing more peace and unspeakable joy. Look for a moment at the question that Paul asks of those in Galatia. "Am I now trying to win the approval of human beings, or of God? Or am I trying to please men? If I were still trying to please men, I would not be a servant of Christ" (Galatians 1:10 NIV). Consider this translation. "For do I now persuade men, or

God? Or do I seek to please men? For if I yet pleased men, I should not be the servant of Christ" (Galatians 1:10 KJV).

When we are looking to fit into the world, the tendency is to be very organized, accommodating, helpful, and supportive, even when we don't have time. You are hoping that your friends, family, or co-workers will view you as a real team player because of the sacrifices made to your own detriment. You are a pleasure to spend time with because you do so much to make life easy for others.

While these behaviors represent your outside face, there is usually a different dialogue on the inside. That's why you feel fake. You know that there is another conversation happening, and that the motive for what you do is not as pure as it may seem.

Here are some of the thoughts and feelings you or others struggling to be real may have:

- Fear of loss of approval
- Fear of rejection
- Fear of loss of personal identity
- Fear of loss of personal worth
- Denial of problems
- Self-denial or ignoring of personal rights
- Feeling lonely and isolated from others
- Feeling the need to avoid conflicts or fights at any cost
- Feeling not "good enough"
- Feeling undeserving
- Feeling inferior to others
- Concern about satisfying others' demands

- Insecurity about personal abilities, skills, or knowledge
- Confusion about why it takes so much energy to please others
- Fear of letting their friends and family down
- Fear of failure
- Fear of being "found out" you are not as good as you appear to others
- Desire to run away to avoid the stress of always needing to be good
- Exhaustion from always trying to be "perfect"
- Disappointment in not being able to make everyone happy
- Feeling unappreciated, taken advantage of, or taken for granted

When these things preoccupy your thoughts and emotions, it is difficult to feel like a real person. These negative thoughts and emotions will affect your entire life—your self-esteem, your identity, and your outlook. The consequences? Inability to make wise judgments, poor problem-solving abilities, stress, and burnout.

The picture I paint may be worse than how you are currently feeling, but if you don't look into the mirror of God's Word and quickly change your opinion of yourself to what God says, this is where you are headed. You will find yourself unable to appreciate what God has given you and unable to accept kindnesses from others.

My dear sister, you are a real person. Stop believing the lies of the world that keep you in bondage and lead to acting out behaviors such as substance abuse and revealing clothing that draw the wrong kind of attention.

Here are just a few of the lies women often believe:

- I must be liked by everyone.
- I must not do anything to upset others.
- People would never like me if they knew the truth about me.
- I can never do enough to please them.
- I am responsible for other people's happiness.
- If people do not like me, then I must be no good.
- People can only like you if you appear nice, pleasant, friendly, and cheerful to them.
- If you are not successful, you are a loser and losers are ignored, unloved, and unwanted.
- It's not who you are but what you do that counts.
- No matter what I do, it never seems to be "good enough."
- I can do nothing right. I am worthless, useless, but I cannot let others see this about me or they will reject me.

Believe the Word of God and follow the example of the apostle Paul. In everything that he did for those at the church in Thessalonica he was able to remind them that his motives were pure. He was not looking to please anyone other than God; he was not being a fake, but a real person.

For the appeal we make does not spring from error or impure motives, nor are we trying to trick you. On the contrary, we speak as men approved by God to be entrusted with the gospel. We are not trying to please men, but God, who tests our hearts. You know we never used flattery, nor did we put on a mask to cover up greed—God is our witness. We were not looking for praise from men, not from you or anyone else. (1 Thessalonians 2:3–6 NIV)

Q: I have been working for a major corporation for twenty years. I started in the secretarial pool, continued my education, and I now have my master's degree in Business Administration. All of the young men that started with the company when I did are now in higher positions than me. I thought this was strange as they have bachelor's degrees and this company promotes on the basis of educational levels. Last week I overheard the CEO and other leaders talking with some of these young men about promoting me as their token female before there was trouble because there were other women coming up in the ranks with more education than they had. When I heard them all laugh, I was shocked and angry. I thought the CEO valued me as an employee. Now I don't know what to do. I need my job, but I don't think I can keep working here unless I confront them, and then I may still lose my job. What should I do? Signed: Not Valued

A: Dear Not Valued,

You say that the CEO does not value you; have you asked for a promotion and been denied or did you wait passively to be noticed? Did you seek and pursue higher positions as you became qualified? Career women are accused of being too aggressive, but I fear you have not been aggressive or assertive enough.

Yes, a talk with the CEO about the policies in making promotions will be a step in the right direction (whether it is up the ladder or out the door). Think of the women coming behind you. If no one speaks up, nothing will change. Just remember to remain respectful and professional. Do not become emotional and stay factual. You may be amazed at the change in your workplace.

There is an implication, both in the church and in the world, that women are not supposed to be in positions of authority or leadership. They are not chairperson/founder/visionary material. Where in the world or rather who in the world came up with this "supposed to be" list? So many of us women and men have swallowed these lines hook, line, and sinker, but are they true or false? Let's pause and really take a good look at them.

Test your knowledge about strong women; are these statements true or false?

1. Women are not supposed to be strong, stable, and secure.
2. A strong woman has to be handled and kept in check.
3. Women are not supposed to be in a leadership position.
4. A strong woman will dominate, emasculate, and castrate a man.
5. A strong woman cannot honor her husband nor follow his lead.
6. A strong woman cannot be sensitive, spiritual, and supportive.

It is my hope that you realize all the statements above are false.

In my travels around the world, I often encounter women who are struggling with their positions of leadership, their calling, and their gifting because of what other people say they are supposed to be or not supposed to be doing. Many of these powerful women in leadership not only have issues with the perceptions of others, but also relationship concerns with male counterparts.

God tells all of us, men and women alike, to "be strong in the Lord and in the strength of His might" (Ephesians 6:10). We are told to be bold and be strong for the Lord our God is with us (Joshua 1:9).

When our identity is rooted in Christ, not in our education, background, or experiences, we can be secure in our significance. We can know that we are fearfully and wonderfully made and know that right well (Psalm 139:14). Having credentials that acknowledge our credibility is important but it is God that exalts, gives promotion, and opens a door of opportunity that no man can shut (Revelation 3:8).

God has given the gift of leadership to women as well as men. The Bible gives us many examples of women in leadership such as Deborah (Judges 4; 5:7), Queen Esther (The Book of Esther), Mary the Mother of Jesus (Luke 1), Priscilla the missionary, and Zelophehad's four daughters who were leaders in changing the law of the land with God's approval (Numbers 27:1–7). These women were all placed in leadership positions by God, who cannot be wrong and cannot make a mistake. God made women to fill whatever position or place He has destined for them.

Understanding this will help your progression forward as a mover and shaker, impacting the world for the kingdom.

LET US PRAY

Dear Lord, you have made me in your image. Thank you! Help me to remember this one fact when I start to think that I am not good enough, not smart enough, not pretty enough, until I feel paralyzed. Lord, I pray that you will help me to renew my mind as I study your Word. I know that I am who you say I am. Help me to be strong against the ways of the world. Please help me and teach me to listen only to your voice, and to obey your Word. Lord, thank you for reminding me that outward beauty fades, but you look at our hearts. Keep my heart clean and pure. Help me to carry myself like your daughter, someone that is precious and honored in your sight. Help me to neither think lowly of myself nor be haughty, but instead to be sober-minded about who I am in you. I am so blessed that you have made me, formed me, and shaped me. Thank you. In Jesus' name, amen!

Scripture Truth to Help You LIVE RIGHT NOW

Category: SELF-IMAGE

So God created man in his own image, in the image of God he created him; male and female he created them.

Genesis 1:27 (ESV)

But the LORD said to Samuel, "Do not look on his appearance or on the height of his stature, because I have rejected him. For the LORD sees not as man sees: man looks on the outward appearance, but the LORD looks on the heart."

1 Samuel 16:7 (ESV)

For You formed my inward parts; You covered me in my mother's womb. I will praise You, for I am fearfully and wonderfully made; marvelous are Your works, and that my soul knows very well. My frame was not hidden from You, when I was made in secret, and skillfully wrought in the lowest parts of the earth.

Psalm 139:13–15 (NKJV)

Charm is deceitful and beauty is passing, but a woman who fears the LORD, she shall be praised.

Proverbs 31:30 (NKJV)

But now, O LORD, You are our Father; we are the clay, and You our potter; and all we are the work of Your hand.

Isaiah 64:8 (NKJV)

For I know the thoughts that I think toward you, says the LORD, thoughts of peace and not of evil, to give you a future and a hope.

Jeremiah 29:11 (NKJV)

Not that we are sufficient of ourselves to think of anything as being from ourselves, but our sufficiency is from God.

2 Corinthians 3:5 (NKJV)

But we all, with unveiled face, beholding as in a mirror the glory of the Lord, are being transformed into the same image from glory to glory, just as by the Spirit of the Lord.

2 Corinthians 3:18 (NKJV)

Therefore, if anyone is in Christ, he is a new creation; old things have passed away; behold, all things have become new.

2 Corinthians 5:17 (NKJV)

For we dare not class ourselves or compare ourselves with those who commend themselves. But they, measuring themselves by themselves, and comparing themselves among themselves, are not wise.

2 Corinthians 10:12 (NKJV)

For we are his workmanship, created in Christ Jesus for good works, which God prepared beforehand, that we should walk in them.

Ephesians 2:10 (ESV)

Do not let your adorning be external—the braiding of hair and the putting on of gold jewelry, or the clothing you wear—but let your adorning be the hidden person of the heart with the imperishable beauty of a gentle and quiet spirit, which in God's sight is very precious.

1 Peter 3:3–4 (ESV)

Live the Word. Live Right Now Application

Select five verses about self-image from the previous pages and complete these exercises.

Verse # 1 _____

How would you summarize this verse of Scripture?

_____

_____

_____

What does the Bible verse mean to you? _____

_____

_____

_____

Does this verse give you instructions for hope, help, or healing?

_____

As you read this verse of Scripture, do you feel the need to repent, reflect, or rejoice? _____

What do you need to do differently to live right now?

_____

_____

Name at least one person to whom you can be accountable and share your decision to live right now.

_____

Name at least one person you can encourage by sharing this Scripture. _____

Verse # 2 _____

How would you summarize this verse of Scripture?

_____

_____

_____

What does the Bible verse mean to you? _____

_____

_____

Does this verse give you instructions for hope, help, or healing?

_____

As you read this verse of Scripture, do you feel the need to repent, reflect, or rejoice? _____

What do you need to do differently to live right now?

_____

_____

Name at least one person to whom you can be accountable and share your decision to live right now.

_____

Name at least one person you can encourage by sharing this Scripture. _____

Verse # 3 _____

How would you summarize this verse of Scripture?

_____

_____

_____

_____

What does the Bible verse mean to you? _____

_____

_____

_____

Does this verse give you instructions for hope, help, or healing?

_____

As you read this verse of Scripture, do you feel the need to repent, reflect, or rejoice? _____

What do you need to do differently to live right now?

_____

_____

Name at least one person to whom you can be accountable and share your decision to live right now.

_____

Name at least one person you can encourage by sharing this Scripture. _____

Verse # 4 _____

How would you summarize this verse of Scripture?

_____

_____

_____

What does the Bible verse mean to you? _____

_____

_____

Does this verse give you instructions for hope, help, or healing?

_____

As you read this verse of Scripture, do you feel the need to repent, reflect, or rejoice? _____

What do you need to do differently to live right now?

_____

_____

Name at least one person to whom you can be accountable and share your decision to live right now.

_____

Name at least one person you can encourage by sharing this Scripture. _____

Verse # 5 _____

How would you summarize this verse of Scripture?

_____

_____

_____

What does the Bible verse mean to you? _____

_____

_____

Does this verse give you instructions for hope, help, or healing?

_____

As you read this verse of Scripture, do you feel the need to repent, reflect, or rejoice? _____

What do you need to do differently to live right now?

_____

_____

Name at least one person to whom you can be accountable and share your decision to live right now.

_____

Name at least one person you can encourage by sharing this Scripture.

_____

CHAPTER 7

FINANCIAL MATTERS

Give me five minutes with a person's checkbook, and I will tell you where their heart is.

Billy Graham

And my God shall supply all your need according to His riches in glory by Christ Jesus.

Philippians 4:19 (NKJV)

All throughout your life you have probably heard many messages about money, from spending and saving to debt and credit. There are lessons to learn on budgeting, tithing, investing, and retirement. Most of what we know about money management we learned from our parents, the media, or the church. Like other areas in our lives, we have only partial information that ends up not being truth at all. And of course, when you hear a lie often enough, you start to believe it. For example, have you ever heard someone say, "Money is the root of all evil"? Well, that is not what the Bible says.

The Bible is not against money itself nor is it against the lawful possession of money, even in large amounts. It is not money that is at the root of all evil, despite the fact that a great many people misquote the apostle Paul's words (1 Timothy 6:10). It is the love of money that is at the root of all evil. The love of money can lead to greed, dishonesty, and get-rich-quick schemes that take advantage of others. Conversely, the lack of money can lead to discontentment, envy, and compromise.

> **Money is neutral. What really matters is the heart of the person who has it and whether he or she has chosen to live right with God's provisions.**

When it comes to finances, the Word of God has much to say. Different sources say the number of Bible verses pertaining to money is as low as 1,100 and as high as 2,000. Whatever is the actual count, we can be clear that the Word is not silent about the matter. We need an abundance of biblical information to help combat the onslaught of worldly views about how we should manage the resources that God has provided. There are also numerous Christian authors who have written in depth on the subject of financial peace and money management such as Larry Burkett, Randy Alcorn, Ron Blue, and Dave Ramsey. These guys know that there is a plan for our money and help us to remember to apply it.

It is often clear by the way we make plans with the finances we have that we have forgotten that it is God who gives us the power and the ability to create wealth (Deuteronomy 8:18). We are only stewards over the resources (1 Corinthians 4:1–2). Because the world believes money answers all things, we tend to depend on money more than we depend on God. We look at what we can buy versus what is really important.

Consider the words of this adage that I heard a long time ago.

Money can buy a house but not a home.
Money can buy a bed but not sleep.
Money can buy a book but not knowledge.
Money can buy a clock but not time.
Money can buy medicine but not health.
Money can buy position but not respect.
Money can buy blood but not life.
Money can buy sex but not love.
Money can buy insurance but not safety.
Money can buy food but not an appetite.

Slick advertising, fancy graphics, and catchy jingles can lead you to believe otherwise. It's hard to imagine that life can be happy with little. However, when we are faithful to God, He can cause increase and what we have becomes more than enough for us and to share. There are several verses in Proverbs that speak of the peace one can have even with little money.

Better is little with the fear of the LORD, than great treasure with trouble.

Proverbs 15:16 (NKJV)

Better is a little with righteousness than great revenues with injustice.

Proverbs 16:8 (ESV)

Better is a dry morsel with quietness, than a house full of feasting with strife.

Proverbs 17:1 (NKJV)

Most of us don't handle money very well. It can be problematic if we are wealthy or if we are poor. Remember, money is neutral. What really matters is the heart of the person who has it and whether he or she has chosen to live right with God's provisions. Listen to what the apostle Paul told the brethren in Philippians 4:12: "I know what it is to be in need, and I know what it is to have plenty. I have learned the secret of being content in any and every situation, whether well fed or hungry, whether living in plenty or in want" (NIV). Scripture teaches:

- Money can be used for great good (i.e., feeding the hungry; clothing the naked; building hospitals, schools, and churches)—Luke 10:30–37.

- Money can be used for great evil (i.e., pornography, prostitution, drugs, alcohol, gambling) —1 Timothy 6:10.

- Money if not used properly (Matthew 6:19–24) can be a curse instead of a blessing and lead to terrible bondage (Proverbs 22:7).

- Money must be used to bring glory to God—1 Corinthians 10:31. When our money is properly used, we are privileged to see the hand of God at work as He provides for His people (Malachi 3:8–12).

In Proverbs 3:9–10, we find this command: "Honor the LORD from your wealth and from the first of all your produce;

so your barns will be filled with plenty and your vats will overflow with new wine." We are expected to be generous and ready to share. Proverbs 11:24–28 tells us:

> There is one who scatters, and yet increases all the more, and there is one who withholds what is justly due, and yet it results only in want. The generous man will be prosperous, and he who waters will himself be watered. He who withholds grain, the people will curse him, but blessing will be on the head of him who sells it . . . He who trusts in his riches will fall, but the righteous will flourish like the green leaf.

Listed below are four common statements about finances that can even cause Christians to be distracted.

- There is just not enough money to go around so I cannot think about giving.
- My money belongs to me to do with it as I please.
- If only I had more money, then I'd be happy (which equates to "If I had a bigger house, a nicer car, took big vacations, and could afford the 'finer things in life,' then I'd be happy").
- The only way to get ahead is to beat the system (which might require you to lie, cheat, and/or steal).

When the world's system promotes lies regarding finances and money, don't listen.

Some of you may have fallen prey to the above fallacies. Although it may seem tough, we can handle our money in a way that pleases God. The question is, are you ready to live right in the area of your finances? During challenging economic times, it is imperative that we focus on the family from a biblical perspective so that our families can survive the shifting economy. When money is tight and couples do not have a plan for how to navigate their limited resources, it leads to increased problems in communication such as frustration, accusations, arguments, or sometimes even worse. For each individual it can lead to outbursts of anger, increased worry, anxiety over paying bills and making ends meet, or even depression as you have to cut back and answer bill collectors. The children often become pawns and parents may feel guilty that they are not able to give their children as much as they would like as they find it more and more difficult to keep up with what others have in the neighborhood or at school.

For couples that have a hard time navigating their finances, a healthy sex life is usually out of the question. Working extra hours and/or two jobs apiece to make ends meet may lead to exhaustion and limited time for intimacy due to scheduling. This may sound all too familiar. It may represent your household or someone you know and care about.

There is hope! God is able. Discipline is possible. You can survive the economy. Families of faith do not have to become part of the negative national statistics, because God is the major denominator in all of our equations. When we focus on our families in accordance to the Word, God will add wisdom, multiply our limited resources, subtract unwise decisions that lead to debt, and keep the enemy's attacks at bay.

The Lord has given us the ability to create wealth. Christian financial advice is practical and includes proven tips, tools, and techniques rooted in the Bible. Christian financial advice stresses Jesus' words in Matthew 16:26: "What good will it be for a man if he gains the whole world, yet forfeits his soul?" (NIV). Below are a few practical tips for getting a handle on your finances:

> **Money is the substance but God is the source.**

Eliminate the waste. Quit paying large sums of money for things that are rarely used—expensive toys that sit in the corner, things for hobbies that you never took up. Get only what you need; don't try to keep up with the Joneses or the media hype. Get rid of those unused items that you have and convert them into cash.

Decrease your debt. Month after month families keep adding to their debt. We need a reversal of fortune—decreased spending and increased saving. Starting the process is simpler than you might imagine. Initiate your own spending freeze; put the reins on all spending until you document where every penny is going. Spend on items that are absolutely necessary like food, water, and shelter. This will be a time of no frills; you may even want to fast and pray. Designate the money saved toward reducing the debt. You will not get out of debt paying the monthly minimums.

Increase your saving (instead of spending). Monies that are not going toward debt reduction should be going to the bank. In addition, everyone in the house should have an old-fashioned piggy bank. The goal should be for the pig to get fat for the slaughter. The collection of loose change can change how you view money. Pennies become dollars quickly if you let them add up and don't spend them. Focus on long-term goals instead of immediate gratification.

Increase your giving. Some of the money that you save because of the changes you are making should be diverted to the kingdom. Have a need? Plant a seed.

It is amazing the difference getting control of your finances will make in your life. Less money will be wasted so you may find you don't have to work as long (or hard) to make ends meet. That means you'll have more time to spend on the important things in your life. Your stress level will most likely decrease in direct proportion to the decrease in bickering over family money.

We forfeit a great blessing when we are not obedient to God's Word. He wants us to bring Him glory as we provide for our families and advance His kingdom. We demonstrate faith in His promises by our giving, we expose ourselves to His blessings, and we do something in which everyone can participate. We find this instruction in 1 Timothy 6:17–19:

> Instruct those who are rich in this present world not to be conceited or to fix their hope on the uncertainty of riches, but on God, who richly supplies us with all things to enjoy. Instruct them to do good, to be rich in good works, to be generous and ready to share, storing up for themselves the treasure of a good foundation for the future, so that they may take hold of that which is life indeed.

It is amazing to see this principle played out over and over again in our lives. If you are generous even when you have little, God blesses your finances to be able to do more than most who have more money than you. We constantly hear and read about people who recovered from massive amounts of debt while staying faithful to giving. Even those who don't believe in God understand the value and importance of giving back and the increase we receive as we are a blessing to others. Money is the substance but God is the source.

God's Word on finances is truth for everyone who applies the principles. Many books have been written on the subject to help believers live right. Although the challenges may vary, God's Word is constant. He wants you to experience abundance and be a good steward of the wealth. As you exercise God's wisdom in financial matters, you will build wealth for yourself and the generations who come after you.

Q: My household is wonderful, but not everyone would agree. My husband and I were married after we were both in our late thirties. We knew I was making more money than he was, and it would probably stay that way. We decided we were fine with that, and we would start our family right away. We decided my husband would work until the baby was born. Then he would stay home and I would go back to work, because my salary was enough for us to live comfortably. We now have two children and this is working well for us, but not for others. His family is very angry. They say I have emasculated him. His male friends joke and tease him about being a househusband. We are happy with our arrangement, and our children are well cared for and happy. However, all this talk is wearing him down. He has started to talk about finding another job. I worry what will happen if he doesn't find something soon. What if it doesn't pay as much as I currently make, which is a significant salary? Why can't people let us live our lives? Signed: Don't Mess with My Household

A: Dear Don't Mess with My Household,

If what you and your husband decided lines up with God's best for the two of you and the children, then stand your ground. You and your husband should not allow others to determine what is in your best interest. You cannot live your life attempting to please others. Your husband should stand up to his parents—respectfully, of course—and inform them that the two of you make decisions based on what's in your best interest. He should explain that while he appreciates their concerns, they have to accept the decisions made by you and your husband.

People should allow you and your husband to live your lives. The two of you must inform them that while they mean well, they are infringing on your marriage. Thank them for their concern and continue to do things as you have in the past. Living to please others can be a constant strain. If your husband finds a job he is not pleased with, it could result in a backlash against you. As you know, frustration is often taken out on the person closest to you. It would be great if your husband could learn to laugh and joke along with his friends and not allow their jokes to get the best of him. Limit the things you discuss with others. People, including family members, should not be privy to how you run your home. Remember, you and your husband made a decision together. As long as you align with the Word of God, nothing else matters.

Q: My sister and her family have lost everything they worked hard to earn the last twenty-two years. They both lost their jobs and lived for the last four years on their retirement. My family is well off financially, yet spiritually my husband "leaves salvation and praying to your God," as he says, to me. I cannot sit and watch my sister lose everything, but my husband makes all the money. He just does not seem to understand why helping them is important or necessary. I feel that if we do not help, then we are not appreciating the blessings that God has provided for us. My husband says he did it all. Signed: Want to Be My Sister's Keeper

A: Dear Want to Be My Sister's Keeper,

Yes, you want to be your sister's keeper. But you are not your own. You have become one with your husband. Therefore, your I is now we. The money does not belong to you alone, but it is a provision that your husband has made to care for his immediate family. It is admirable to want to help your sister, but how will it help your sister to save her household if it tears up yours?

As your biblical sister's keeper, you can pray that the Lord sends another Good Samaritan. It would be destructive for you to go above and beyond what your husband is willing to do. Do not feel guilty about her predicament and do other things that will violate your conscience or create relational losses and poverty at your house. Your husband will be blessed to have you submit to his leading as head of your house.

Through loving conversations (not demands), at a later date maybe you can make an appeal to offer some assistance. Your husband can help bail your sister's family out, but he cannot sustain them. In this economic climate, they may not be able to maintain their current level of living. Trust your sister and her family to the Lord. Then do what you are able to do with your husband's approval as often as you can.

Q: I am a well-educated and skilled person who is over 40 and having a challenging time obtaining gainful employment that will pay at the level to which I am accustomed. With my two kids, I am having a hard time making ends meet. I believe in God and go to church; yet, I question when the pastor says "the Lord will provide." How can you say that God provides and I am underemployed having to depend on the government for food? Is God really providing and I don't see it? Am I missing the understanding of how God provides? Please help. I need clarity and a better job. Signed: Will God Provide?

A: Dear Will God Provide?

These are challenging days for so many of us. The job market is weak but getting stronger every day. It is wonderful that you have a good education and had a job that paid well. Continue to fellowship with other believers and trust God. Sometimes things happen in our lives that take us by surprise. They try our faith and rock our world. Just remember our God cares for us and He is sovereign. He knows our past, present, and future. He has provision ready for us before the need arises.

God truly is Jehoveh-jireh. This name for God means "The Lord will provide." He has brought you this far by faith (Genesis 22:1–14). Don't keep looking at your circumstances and what you do not have; look at a God who is not only able but willing to supply all of your needs through whatever means He chooses. Your education and your job were just channels through which God blessed you. God will provide. He has already provided for you salvation. He has provided for you the ability to have peace that passes understanding. You can have joy even when you don't know how God will answer your prayers. God has provided good health and skills for employment. God has provided housing and food for you and your children. Yes, God really is providing.

Q: I am 63 years old and have lived my entire life for the Lord. I am a widow of three years and just met a remarkable man of God. The only real challenge is his limited income. To say that my husband left me well taken care of would be an understatement. The caveat is that his funds are tied into me remaining single. I love this man I met but I cannot see myself living on just my retirement and his income. I want to live with him. How can this happen and I stay in the will of God? Signed: I've Got Two Lovers

A: Dear I've Got Two Lovers,

After being faithful to the Lord for 63 years; do you think you will really be happy in an adulterous relationship? You stated, and I quote, "I want to live with him. How can this happen and I stay in the will of God?" The answer is very simple: marry him! If you live with this man without marrying him, you will be out of the will of God and cause those around you to question your walk with God. It is clear that you love God, now which do you love most: your late husband's money or the remarkable man of God? Luke 16:13 tells us, "No one can serve two masters. Either you will hate the one and love the other, or you will be devoted to the one and despise the other. You cannot serve both God and money" (NIV). It's your choice; you can't have it both ways, He is a jealous God and will not be your second lover. Compromise is not the answer; hold fast to your convictions.

Q: My children's father is a deadbeat! First he doesn't pay his child support consistently and I have to go to court constantly to get them to put the pressure on him to pay. Now I have to try to budget my pay with the lack of his contribution to make ends meet. It is hard! I am so frustrated! I am making sacrifices and trying to keep my kids fed and clothed. How do I live on a budget and trust that God is going to make a way for me with so little money? Signed: More Kids Than Money

A: Dear More Kids Than Money,

Being a single parent is not easy even with enough money. Don't use any more energy on the absent father; leave that to the courts—and an attorney if that becomes necessary. Focus your attention on God and your children. Look to God as the source of your supply. You can trust Him; He is faithful! You may need help with making a budget; just be sure to involve your children. Let them help you and be a part of making things better for all of you. God has ways to provide for us that we know nothing about, and He is not helped nor hindered by the amount of money we have or don't have. .

Q: How do I witness to members of my family when each one thinks their Ph.D. knowledge and skill enabled them to be successful? My family advocates education above Christianity. They believe Christianity is for those who are weak and are followers instead of leaders. They do not need the prosperity message; they are rolling in money and see no need to believe in a God somewhere in the imaginary heaven. Signed: Too Smart and Too Rich for God

A: Dear Too Smart and Too Rich for God,

Share the plan of salvation with them. The prosperity message and the message of the gospel are different, so just keep the gospel plain and simple. Tell them even educated people will not be exempt from the trials of life. Their station in life will not prevent them from getting sick or going broke. They may get old and they will surely die. Therefore, they will need God. They need God not only in death but in life.

Everything they have—including their lives—has all been given by God. The abilities they possess and the successes they have achieved are gifts from God, even though they don't see it now. There are things money cannot buy and education cannot help you understand: peace of mind, health, joy, and forgiveness. You can also witness through your personal testimony; your attitude to life's challenges can be the "bible" they read. Serve as a constant witness. Walk the walk, talk the talk, and give thanks in all things.

Q: I have five adult children who are in my pocket! I have given to help them over and over again, and I am tired of it! As parents we need to be helping our offspring to understand and appreciate money and wealth. We need to help them become good stewards. I did not have that coming up and, of course, I did not pass it to my children. But I want them to be more than sufficient in handling their money. I would like my grandchildren to come to be wiser with their finances. Please tell me how I can redirect my children and be prepared to train our future generations to manage finances God's way. Signed: Get Them Out of My Pocket

A: Dear Get Them Out of My Pocket,

It sounds as if you are on your way to financial freedom from your children. I agree that it is important to teach your children the value of money and to become good stewards. Even if you did not have this training when you were a child, what you are learning now can still be passed on to your children. There are many great books on handling finances God's way by authors such as Larry Burkett, Ron Blue, and Dave Ramsey. There also programs and classes that you and your children can take together like Crown Ministries or Financial Peace University.

As the parent of these five adult children, you will need to set some realistic limits and loving boundaries on distribution of funds to this group. If you no longer plan to be the Mom Bank and Trust, then hold a family meeting and let them know about the changes you are preparing to make. Adult children who have personal luxuries and expect parents to pay the bills or cover their housing expenses will have a hard time adjusting. When children are struggling and need occasional assistance, it is permissible to help, but you should not create a welfare system or monthly revolving door. If you are financially stable and in a position to help your adult children who are truly in need, then be a blessing to them. Be careful not to set up an unhealthy cycle of dependence.

I don't know what has happened between you and your children as it relates to finances, but you sound like you are at your limit. Helping them should not be hurting you. Families do take care of each other but should not take advantage of each other. Likewise, those who are truly in need should not suffer because of those who have abused the privileges you have graciously extended. Pray for your children, help only when the need is genuine, encourage them to secure biblical financial education, and be there to teach your grandchildren.

Q: The Bible says "the wealth of the sinner is laid up for the just" (Proverbs 13:22 KJV) and that "It is [God] who gives you the power to get wealth" (Deuteronomy 8:18 ESV). If this is true, how do I need to position myself and my family to receive or create wealth? There are so many get-rich speakers, programs, and scams out there. I see how they get rich; all of us poor working people give them our money for their products. What is the true formula to wealth? Is this biblical wealth all about money or am I missing the meaning? Whatever you share will help me plan for my family. I have four young children that I hope will live a better life than mine. Is the Bible real on the topic of wealth? Signed: Help Me Get Wealth

A: Dear Help Me Get Wealth,

There is no *if* to the Bible; there is an *if,* however, to our behavior. The Bible is true and if we apply the principles to our behavior we receive the benefits. Just about everyone wants the "wealth of the sinner that is laid up for the just." The beginning of that verse in Proverbs 13:22 states that, "A good man leaves an inheritance for his children's children." This person is not just waiting to collect the wealth of sinners but he is working and making plans for generations to come. In Ecclesiastes 2:26 we are told, "To the man who pleases him, God gives wisdom, knowledge and happiness, but to the sinner he gives the task of gathering and storing up wealth to hand it over to the one who pleases God. This too is meaningless, a chasing after the wind" (NIV). The Bible does not give directions for positioning yourself for wealth, but it gives much wisdom on how to get wealth, keep wealth, share wealth, and do good with your wealth. The true formula for wealth is found in the Bible. Consider the following verses. I believe that a careful study of these with your children will help you experience great wealth:

- Therefore do not be anxious, saying, 'What shall we eat?' or 'What shall we drink?' or 'What shall we wear?' For the Gentiles seek after all these things, and your heavenly Father knows that you need them all. But seek first the kingdom of God and his righteousness, and all these things will be added to you. Matthew 6:31–34 (ESV)

- All hard work brings a profit, but mere talk leads only to poverty. Proverbs 14:23 (NIV)

- Lazy people are soon poor; hard workers get rich. Proverbs 10:4 (NLT)

- The earnings of the godly enhance their lives, but evil people squander their money on sin. Proverbs 10:16 (NLT)

- The blessing of the LORD makes a person rich, and he adds no sorrow with it. Proverbs 10:22 (NLT)
- Riches won't help on the day of judgment, but right living can save you from death. Proverbs 11:4 (NLT)

Q: I have to leave my job because I am expecting a baby. My husband is sick and out of work. We are going to move in with his parents or mine. My parents are already overcrowded as my grandparents are living with them. To make matters worse, I don't want to live with Jeff's parents because his mother thinks I am not good enough for him. Please help me; I am at the point of despair. I am even dreading having to tell my husband and my family about the baby. Where is the silver lining? I am getting eyestrain looking for it through my dark situation. Signed: Dark Days and Nights

A: Dear Dark Days and Nights,

There is no need to strain looking for that silver lining. Your help cometh from the Lord. Read and meditate on the word of encouragement found in Psalm 121:1–8. You are a blessed woman to have options in this season of trial and challenge. Caring for and ministering to a sick husband that is unemployed while you have a baby on the way is not for the faint-hearted. God will strengthen you for the days ahead as you lean on Him. This must also be a challenging time for your husband as well. The two of you will need to be of one accord regarding the decisions made about your living arrangement. It is commonplace for couples to move in with family members during economically challenging times. Before you do, however, have an official meeting with the family about dos and don'ts as well as expectations. Sacrifices will be made by both parties. It is also helpful if there is a timeline for how long you plan to be there, even if it is tentative. Your host should know that the arrangements are temporary until you get your finances in order. Also, let all involved know up front about the baby, as that will impact the decision regarding housing. This time of transition does not have to be a strain. It can be a great blessing as generations bond and support one another. This is also a good time to draw closer together and resolve any differences you may have with each other. This will be a chance to practice these verses on relationships:

- Be kind and compassionate to one another, forgiving each other, just as in Christ God forgave you. Ephesians 4:32 (NIV)

- Don't be selfish; don't try to impress others. Be humble, thinking of others as better than yourselves. Philippians 2:3 (NLT)

- A new command I give you: Love one another. As I have loved you, so you must love one another. John 13:34 (NIV)

Thank God for your family and your options; then pray for one another.

LET US PRAY

Father God, you have given me power to get wealth so that I can be used to help establish your covenant in the earth. Help me to use money and not let it use me. Give me wisdom in my financial dealings. Let me be mindful to know that you are my source and that money is just one of the many means. I thank you that the earth is yours and everything in it. I thank you that you own it all and that you allow me to have stewardship over a portion. Thank you for being my provider. Lord, you have shown yourself faithful to me and my family over and over again. God, you have given us what we need and many times even the desires of our hearts. Help me to be wise with the resources you have given. In Jesus' name, amen!

Scripture Truth to Help You LIVE RIGHT NOW

Category: FINANCIAL MATTERS

Remember the LORD your God, for it is he who gives you the ability to produce wealth.

Deuteronomy 8:18 (NIV)

You shall generously give to him, and your heart shall not be grieved when you give to him, because for this thing the LORD your God will bless you in all your work and in all your undertakings.

Deuteronomy 15:10

And you shall again obey the LORD, and observe all His commandments which I command you today. Then the LORD your God will prosper you abundantly in all the work of your hand, in the offspring of your body and in the offspring of your cattle and in the produce of your ground, for the LORD will again rejoice over you for good, just as He rejoiced over your fathers; if you obey the LORD your God to keep His commandments and His statutes which are written in this book of the law, if you turn to the LORD your God with all your heart and soul.

Deuteronomy 30:8–10

This book of the law shall not depart from your mouth, but you shall meditate on it day and night, so that you may be careful to do according to all that is written in it; for then you will make your way prosperous, and then you will have success.

Joshua 1:8

Blessed is the man who does not walk in the counsel of the wicked or stand in the way of sinners or sit in the seat of mockers. But his delight is in the law of the LORD, and on his law he meditates day and night. He is like a tree planted by streams of water, which yields its fruit in season and whose leaf does not wither. Whatever he does prospers.

Psalm 1:1–3 (NIV)

A false balance is an abomination to the LORD, but a just weight is his delight.

Proverbs 11:1 (ESV)

Wealth gained hastily will dwindle, but whoever gathers little by little will increase it.

Proverbs 13:11 (ESV)

Precious treasure and oil are in a wise man's dwelling, but a foolish man devours it.

Proverbs 21:20 (ESV)

Whoever oppresses the poor to increase his own wealth, or gives to the rich, will only come to poverty.

Proverbs 22:16 (ESV)

For he will be like a tree planted by the water, that extends its roots by a stream and will not fear when the heat comes; but its leaves will be green, and it will not be anxious in a year of drought nor cease to yield fruit.

Jeremiah 17:8

"Bring all the tithes into the storehouse, that there may be food in My house, and try Me now in this," says the LORD of hosts, "if I will not open for you the windows of heaven and pour out for you such blessing that there will not be room enough to receive it."

Malachi 3:10 (NKJV)

Beloved, I pray that you may prosper in all things and be in health, just as your soul prospers.

3 John 1:2 (NKJV)

Live the Word. Live Right Now Application

Select five verses about financial matters from the previous pages and complete these exercises.

Verse # 1 _____

How would you summarize this verse of Scripture?

_____

_____

_____

What does the Bible verse mean to you? _____

_____

_____

Does this verse give you instructions for hope, help, or healing?

_____

As you read this verse of Scripture, do you feel the need to repent, reflect, or rejoice? _____

What do you need to do differently to live right now?

_____

_____

Name at least one person to whom you can be accountable and share your decision to live right now.

_____

Name at least one person you can encourage by sharing this Scripture. _____

Verse # 2 _____

How would you summarize this verse of Scripture?

_____

_____

_____

What does the Bible verse mean to you? _____

_____

_____

_____

Does this verse give you instructions for hope, help, or healing?

_____

As you read this verse of Scripture, do you feel the need to repent, reflect, or rejoice? _____

What do you need to do differently to live right now?

_____

_____

Name at least one person to whom you can be accountable and share your decision to live right now.

_____

Name at least one person you can encourage by sharing this Scripture. _____

Verse # 3 _____

How would you summarize this verse of Scripture?

_____

_____

_____

What does the Bible verse mean to you? _____

_____

_____

_____

Does this verse give you instructions for hope, help, or healing?

_____

As you read this verse of Scripture, do you feel the need to repent, reflect, or rejoice? _____

What do you need to do differently to live right now?

_____

_____

Name at least one person to whom you can be accountable and share your decision to live right now.

_____

Name at least one person you can encourage by sharing this Scripture. _____

Verse # 4 _____

How would you summarize this verse of Scripture?

_____

_____

_____

What does the Bible verse mean to you? _____

_____

_____

Does this verse give you instructions for hope, help, or healing?

_____

As you read this verse of Scripture, do you feel the need to repent, reflect, or rejoice? _____

What do you need to do differently to live right now?

_____

_____

Name at least one person to whom you can be accountable and share your decision to live right now.

_____

Name at least one person you can encourage by sharing this Scripture. _____

Verse # 5 _____

How would you summarize this verse of Scripture?

_____

_____

_____

What does the Bible verse mean to you? _____

_____

_____

Does this verse give you instructions for hope, help, or healing?

_____

As you read this verse of Scripture, do you feel the need to repent, reflect, or rejoice? _____

What do you need to do differently to live right now?

_____

_____

Name at least one person to whom you can be accountable and share your decision to live right now.

_____

Name at least one person you can encourage by sharing this Scripture.

_____

CONCLUSION

Every action of our lives takes on some chord that will vibrate in eternity.

Edwin Hubbell Chapin

And you shall know the truth, and the truth shall make you free.

John 8:32 (NKJV)

Declare today as the day to live right, to aspire higher and to make a dynamic impact. Today is more than just another day. It is the day that the Lord has made. It is a day that you have never seen before. It is the day that you were planning for yesterday. It is a day your life will change based on your decision right now to live according to the Word of God. This day is a day of new mercies (Lamentations 3:22–23). This is a day of new landmarks, new opportunities, new relationships, and a new perspective.

This day is more than just another day with the word *new* in front. It really is an opportunity for renewal, growth, expansion, change, and transformation. This day is a clean slate to become all that God has destined and purposed for your life. Begin now being and becoming. Yes, today. It is time for you to declare that you will alter your lifestyle and your life.

We have survived. We have made it through. Some of us battered, broken, or bruised, but we are still here. If you have endured and survived, imagine what those around you have gone through, especially those who were close enough to be impacted by the things that affected you. I am happy to share with you that it doesn't matter what you are going through, what you have gone through, or how far you have gone. There shall be a radical turning in your situation as you embrace God's truth and focus your energies toward the destination the Lord has for your life.

> **There shall be a radical turning in your situation as you embrace God's truth and focus your energies toward the destination the Lord has for your life.**

When you are ready to live right in any of the seven areas discussed in this book, there is hope, help, and healing available. I pray that as you have flipped through the pages you have found yourself nodding in agreement and thinking about what you would have said and may say to those in similar situations. I pray that you will apply the key principles necessary for living the abundant life. When you walk in the Spirit, you do not fulfill the lusts of the flesh.

As we come to the end of this phase of the journey, there are a few things you want to begin doing. For those of you who are Christians, begin an in-depth study of the Word to help you grow and be able to provide counsel for others who are struggling to live right as they go through life.

Make some clear decisions about your life and your relationship with Christ. If you have been simply going to church and not really reading and applying the Word to your daily life, start today. If you have been sitting in the pews and have not accepted Jesus Christ as your personal Savior to lead and guide your life, you can make that decision now as you say a prayer, based on the Scriptures:

> **If you confess with your mouth that Jesus is Lord, and believe in your heart that God raised Him from the dead, you will be saved. Romans 10:9 (NLT)**

Father, I confess that Jesus is Lord, and I believe you raised Him from the dead. I believe in you, Lord Jesus, and I ask you to be my Lord and Savior. Thank you for giving me the right to become your child.

As we repent, let go, and move on, the blessings of the Lord shall overtake us. The newness that we so desire can begin today. Redemption has been provided. We need to reconnect to the things that matter most (the Lord and our families), we need to reconcile to one another, restore broken relationships through forgiveness, and we need to remember the goodness of the Lord so that we share with others the testimony of His faithfulness.

I overheard a conversation where someone was indicating that they were looking forward to the New Year because business was bad due to the failing economy. Before the person could finish, he was challenged to reconsider his thoughts. "Despite the economy," the friend replied, "You have good health, peace of mind, joy, and the love of family. What have you done with all this time that the Lord has graciously given you? Did you work on pending projects? Did you spend time with family and friends? Did you witness and draw people into the kingdom?" As I listened I asked myself these same questions. Now, I'll ask you.

Last year the news focused on layoffs, foreclosures, setbacks, and upheavals. But the one thing that has remained constant through it all is the love of God. Because He loves us, He has neither left us nor forsaken us. He is with us as we struggle with our relationships, church and religion, emotional healing, sex and sexuality, parenting, self-image, and yes, even our financial matters.

> *To all who received him, to those who believed in his name, he gave the right to become children of God. John 1:12 (NIV)*

Many will wait until January 1 to begin changing. But when we wait, we allow things to linger in our lives that need to be removed. When we wait, we postpone the abundance that God has in store for us. Even when things are going good, they can be better. And certainly if you have had a challenging year like many others, you are ready for change, a new start, a New Year. Are you ready? Then say so:

I declare today is more than just another day, it is the beginning of my New Year.

I declare this is the day that the Lord has made.

I declare today is a day of new mercies (Lamentations 3:22–23).

I declare today is a clean slate to become all that God has destined for my life.

I declare today is an opportunity for renewal and growth.

I declare today is a day of expansion, change, and transformation.

I declare today is my set time to change and alter my lifestyle.

I declare today my life will change as I obey the Word of God.

I declare today is a day of new landmarks, opportunities, relationships, and perspectives.

I declare today that I am ready to live right!

As you prepare to begin your New Year today, what do you need to shift or change in order to accomplish all that is set before you? Having a New Year is more than just coming up with a catchy theme or making a list of resolutions that we so often neglect by the end of the first month. Having a New Year is more about reflecting on where you have been, realizing where you are now, and recognizing the potential you have in God to aspire higher and make a dynamic impact on the people around you.

You make a difference.

Whether you are a mother, father, sister, brother, daughter, son, sister-, or brother-in-law—you matter. Friend, co-worker, colleague, congregant—they are in your circle of influence too. The lives you touch can be transformed based on your interaction. When we are challenged by the issues of life, we can easily forget that we matter to so many people. A word from the Lord that you share with a friend in Baltimore can impact that person's cousin in Atlanta or her sister in Afghanistan.

When we are more conscious of our impact, we can be more intentional and aspire higher to give more, love more, achieve more, and do more for the Lord.

What does it mean to aspire higher? It means to have a great ambition or an ultimate goal that you desire strongly and will strive to achieve. When you are focused, you soar toward that accomplishment. There are five key areas, or impact principles, that will help you experience higher heights and deeper depths as you prepare for transformation in your New Year that starts today. These principles are intercessory prayer, identifying potential, intellectual pursuit, indwelling passion, and intentional preparation.

> *"He asked, 'Sirs, what must I do to be saved?' They replied, 'Believe in the Lord Jesus, and you will be saved.'"*
> **Acts 16:30–31 (NIV)**

Intercessory prayer

Seek God. Usually when change is necessary, we can identify what everyone around us needs to do. Intercessory prayer is about seeking God on their behalf that they might be able to do what is necessary; but also being prepared to be an answer to that prayer by providing help or guidance. As an intercessor we seek God on behalf of others and pray His blessings upon them.

Identifying potential

God has given each of us skills, abilities, and gifts. We need to pray and ask God to help us identify those skills, abilities, or gifts He has given us. As a parent, spouse, family member, or friend, we need to consistently strive to identify the potential in others. We can then encourage one another and use our gifts to work together to the glory of God and to help grow the kingdom of God.

Intellectual pursuit

Continual study and growth are essential for every believer, not just for those currently in school. We should be constantly studying and growing in the things of God. Don't limit yourself to personal devotions alone. Continual growth can be achieved through Bible studies, family devotions, and Christian book clubs. Be creative in your approach to intellectual pursuit; think outside the box for new and exciting ways to study and grow.

Indwelling passion

God has given each of us an indwelling passion. It is simply the thing you are most passionate about. For some it is missions, homeless persons, or youth. It is out of your indwelling passion that ministry is born. What is your indwelling passion? Have you made any commitments concerning your passion? If so, praise God! If not, why not? As we go along in our daily lives, we will often have opportunity to help our family members and friends identify their indwelling passion.

Intentional preparation

Dynamic impact doesn't happen by chance, we must be intentional in our approach and preparation. A baseball team whose goal is to get to the World Series will be intentional in their preparation if they are to be successful. Their intentionality begins with the coaches they hire and the players they recruit, and continues with each decision made during the entire season. How can you start today intentionally preparing for work He has called you to do in the future? Do you need to acquire additional training and education? Commit to be intentional in your preparation for God's work from beginning to end.

To aspire higher and live right now is more than just achieving goals; it is making a dynamic impact. I'm already excited about the approaching New Year that you can begin today. This will be the beginning of the year of dynamic impact for you as your life shifts in the five key areas mentioned above. This is your opportunity to shift, change, and be transformed.

I want you to have a great impact in this year and the rest of your life despite what has happened in the past. And if this past year has been a good year for you, then the strategies below will make your New Year even greater as you apply these impact vehicles. Every day you choose to live right, it increases the impact you make. Specific ways to impact people follow.

Share information

Tell others what they need to know to get to the next level. We all have access to some pertinent resource that will make a significant difference in the life of someone else. We need to be willing to share with the global community so that we can all make a global impact. Share the vision and get connected with other like-minded individuals that will network for the kingdom. The information you have received from this book will also be beneficial to helping others live right.

Be an example

How you carry yourself verbally and nonverbally will speak volumes to those around you. You have the ability to transform others when they come in contact with you. When you consistently live right, people will see you as an individual of character and integrity. You become a dynamic force to usher in peace, love, and joy in any situation.

Develop good habits

Habits and routines become part of who we are. As an individual who aspires to do great things, you want to do the things that matter most. Make the fruit of the Spirit a habit in your life; cultivate joy, peace, patience, goodness. Make it a habit to forgive. Make it a habit to give and sacrifice for others. As those who profess Christ, people are watching our lives and expect us to practice what we preach. They don't want to just hear us talk about the Bible or the love of God; they want to see it demonstrated in our lives. Make that demonstration part of your set of habits.

Cultivate a Christlike attitude

"Let this mind be in you, which was also in Christ Jesus" (Philippians 2:5 KJV). This mind was one of hope, help, healing, and humility. Think of and consider the well-being of others. Allow others to go first, to have the biggest and the best. Show deference to those around you. As you give to others, the Lord will continue to give to you because you become a channel of blessing.

Display character

Be responsible, respectful, and resilient. People often say character is what you do when no one is looking, but it is also what you think when God is listening and what you do that is righteous. Being a person of integrity is a great goal. Look to live your life with a higher standard. Living right is about pursing holiness, practicing godliness, and staying on the path of righteousness.

Share your testimony

Sharing your story to help others overcome will lead to an abundant life of fulfilling your kingdom dream. The apostle Paul shared with those at Philippi that all he had been through, God used for good. Lives were being transformed as he endured. You can make the same proclamation. "My brothers, I want you to know that what has happened to me has made more people know about the good news" (Philippians 1:12 WE). My commitment to faith (no matter what I have been through) is listed below. Please join me in this declaration as we prepare to aspire higher and make a dynamic impact living right for Christ.

I experienced both joy and sorrow as I wrote these words on paper knowing that millions of people around the world will read them and be challenged, changed, and/or charged up. Every time I read one of the questions and answers, I wanted to say more, to give additional Scriptures or books to read that would help encourage, enrich, and empower.

There were times when I wanted to cry as I thought about the situations that my sisters were going through and realized that many of them were barely holding on. I can assure you that if you obey the Word of God, your life will be different. You can declare these things with me now. Say out loud:

- I am getting through the TEST to the TESTIMONY
- I know how to move from the MESS to the MESSAGE
- I have learned to grow through the PAIN to the POWER
- I have learned to break through the BONDAGE to BLESSINGS
- No matter what happens (who did what, why)
- I know how to move from being a VICTIM to VICTORIOUS
- I am giving up GUILT for a lifetime of GRACE
- I plan to PROFIT in my PROBLEMS
- I understand that the TOUGH TIMES count TO-WARD maturity
- I have traveled from TRAGEDY to TRIUMPH
- I can shift from SITTING around, to STANDING STRONG in the Lord
- I can help others rise from DARKNESS to DELIVERANCE
- I can move anybody from PITY to PRAISE
- I know that with every NEW MORNING, there are NEW MERCIES and NEW MIRACLES
- I know that God will RISE within me

- I know that when it pours, He REIGNS
- I know that Jesus on my journey gives me JOY and HOPE unshakeable
- I know that as I aspire higher, I can intentionally have IMPACT and INFLUENCE for the kingdom of God
- I know how to LIVE RIGHT as I face life's tough questions
- I can HELP OTHERS when they are ready to live right
- I know how and will begin to LIVE RIGHT NOW!

As you make this declaration, remember it is not a declaration of independence but one of total dependence on God for everything. We will breathe, move, and have our being in Him alone. Our lives will be one of overflow in all of our relationships. We will be a blessing to all we encounter as we make a dynamic impact. Here is the gospel, or good news, for the New Year: The forecast is bright and your future can be glorious. You may have experienced doom and gloom in the past, but prepare yourself even in what has been your darkest hour to receive double for your trouble. Live right now! Start your New Year and begin to experience the double portion of blessing that is your destiny.

FURTHER READING

Relationships

Marriage and In-laws

Boundaries in Marriage by Dr. Henry Cloud and Dr. John Townsend
Can Two Walk Together? by Sabrina D. Black
Can Two Walk Together Bible Study Guide by Sabrina D. Black
His Needs, Her Needs by Willard F. Harley Jr.
Lady In Waiting by Jackie Kendall and Debby Jones
Liberated Through Submission by P. B. Wilson
Love & Respect by Dr. Emerson Eggerichs
Quest for Love by Elisabeth Elliot
Sacred Marriage by Gary Thomas
The Five Love Languages by Gary Chapman
The Power of a Praying Wife by Stormie Omartian
The Remarriage Checkup by Ron Deal and David Olson

Dating

Before You Say "I Do" by H. Norman Wright
Boundaries in Dating by Dr. Henry Cloud and Dr. John Townsend

How to Date and Stay Saved by Kim Brooks
I Kissed Dating Goodbye by Joshua Harris
Knight in Shining Armor by P. B. Wilson
The Five Love Languages, Singles Edition by Gary Chapman

Friends and Friendship

The Friendships of Women by Dee Brestin
How to Get Along with Almost Anyone by H. Norman Wright

Caregiving

Ambushed by Grace by Shelly Beach
Precious Lord, Take My Hand by Shelly Beach

Mentoring and Discipleship

Spiritual Sisterhood: Mentoring Women of Color by Rebecca Osaigbovo
The Master Plan of Evangelism by Robert Coleman
Women Mentoring Women by Vickie Kraft and Gwynne Johnson

Church and Religion

A Handbook for Christian Maturity: 10 Basic Steps Toward Christian Maturity by Bill Bright
Absolute Surrender by Andrew Murray
Basic Christianity by John Stott
Christianity in Crisis by Hank Hanegraaff
Disciplines of the Holy Spirit by Siang-Yang Tan and Douglas Gregg
Discovering God's Will by Jerry Sittser
Evidence that Demands a Verdict by Josh McDowell
Experiencing God by Henry and Richard Blackaby

Faith

A Woman's Guide to Getting Through Tough Times by Quin Sherrer and Ruthanne Garlock

Extraordinary: The Life You're Meant to Live by John Bevere

Foxe's Book of Martyrs by John Foxe

Hinds' Feet on High Places by Hannah Hurnard

How People Grow by Dr. Henry Cloud and Dr. John Townsend

In Light of Eternity by Randy Alcorn

Just Give Me Jesus by Ann Graham Lotz

Knowing God by J. I. Packer

Living by the Book by Howard and William Hendricks

Mere Christianity by C. S. Lewis

Pilgrim's Progress by John Bunyan

Real Worship by Warren W. Wiersbe

Release of the Spirit by Watchman Nee

Secrets of the Vine by Bruce Wilkinson

The Case for Christ by Lee Strobel

The Cost of Discipleship by Dietrich Bonhoeffer

The Disciplined Life by Richard Taylor

The Holy Spirit by Charles Ryrie

The Normal Christian Life by Watchman Nee

What's So Amazing About Grace? by Philip Yancey

Leadership

Help for Your Leadership by Sabrina Black, Christina Dixon, Pamela Hudson, and Brenda Jenkins

Spiritual Authority by Watchman Nee

The 21 Irrefutable Laws of Leadership by John Maxwell

Making Godly Choices

Be What You Are by Warren W. Wiersbe
Becoming the Noble Woman: God's Master Plan for the Ideal Wife and Mother by Anita Young
Lord Change Me by Evelyn Christenson
Movin' on Up by Rebecca Osaigbovo
Seasons of a Woman's Life by Lois Evans
See Yourself as God Sees You by Josh McDowell
Soul Food and Living Water by Yolanda Powell and William J. Powell
The Practice of Godliness by Jerry Bridges

Forgiveness

A Woman's Guide to Breaking Bondages by Quin Sherrer and Ruthanne Garlock
Betrayal's Baby by P. B. Wilson
Forgiveness by John MacArthur
The Gift of Forgiveness by Charles Stanley
The Path to Reconciliation by Neil Anderson
Forgiveness by Gary Inrig

Hard Sayings

Dealing with the Rejection and Praise of Man by Bob Sorge
Hard Sayings of Jesus by F. F. Bruce
Envy: The Enemy Within by Bob Sorge
No More Excuses by Tony Evans
The Bait of Satan by John Bevere

Emotional Healing

Healing for Damaged Emotions by David Seamands

Man's Search for Meaning by Viktor E. Frankl

A Diary of Joseph: A Spiritual Journey Through Time and *Listen: A Symphony of Faith* by Diane Proctor Reeder

Grief and Loss

A Woman's Guide to Breaking Bondages by Quin Sherrer and Ruthanne Garlock

Battlefield of the Mind by Joyce Meyer

Beauty for Ashes by Joyce Meyer

Healing for Damaged Emotions by David Seamonds

Depression/Anxiety

The Anxiety and Phobia Workbook by Edmund J. Bourne

Feeling Good by Dr. David Burns, M.D.

Letting Go of Worry and Anxiety By Pam Vredevelt

Addiction and Recovery

Adult Children of Alcoholics by Janet Geringer Woititz, Ed.D.

The Big Book of Alcoholics Anonymous by Dr. Bob Smith and Bill Wilson

Codependent No More by Melody Beattie

Healing the Shame that Binds You by John Bradshaw

The Wounded Heart by Dan Allender

Domestic Violence

Battered Love by Renita Weems

Anger

A Woman's Guide to Breaking Bondages by Quin Sherrer and Ruthanne Garlock

Anger: Healing a Powerful Emotion in a Healthy Way e-book by Gary Chapman

Stress and Burnout

Margins by Dr. Richard A. Swenson, M.D.

Meditations for Women Who Do Too Much by Anne Wilson Schaef

Sex and Sexuality

Abstinence

Straight Talk With Your Kids About Sex by Josh McDowell
I Kissed Dating Goodbye by Joshua Harris

Adultery

Torn Asunder: Recovering from an Extramarital Affair by Dave Carder

Pornography

Wired for Intimacy: How Pornography Hijacks the Male Brain by William M. Struthers

Sexual Addiction

Prone to Wander by Sabrina D. Black and Lavern A. Harlin
Intimate Issues by Linda Dillow and Lorraine Pintus
Sheet Music: Uncovering the Secrets of Sexual Intimacy in Marriage by Kevin Leman
The Bondage Breaker by Dr. Neil T. Anderson

Parenting

From Toddlers to Teens

Building a Home Full of Grace by John and Susan Yates and Family
Growing Kids God's Way by Gary Ezzo and Anne Marie Ezzo
Shepherding a Child's Heart by Tedd Trip
The Five Love Languages of Teenagers by Gary Chapman
The New Strong-Willed Child by James Dobson
The Power of Believing in Your Child by Miles McPherson
The Smart Stepfamily by Ron Deal
The Way They Learn by Cynthia Ulrich Tobias
Transforming Children into Spiritual Champions by George Barna
Positioning Your Child for Success by Yvonne Posey Gilchrist

Adoption/Foster Care

The Adoption Decision: 15 Things You Want to Know Before Adopting by Laura Christianson
Successful Adoption: A Guide for Christian Families by Natalie Nichols Gillespie

Infertility

It's OK to Cry: Finding Hope When Struggling with Infertility and Miscarriage by Malcolm Cameron and Nick Cameron

Blended Families

Beyond the Brady Bunch: Hope and Help for Blended Families by Ray and Debbie Alsdorf

Grandparenting

The Power of a Godly Grandparent: Leaving a Spiritual Legacy by Stephen and Janet Bly

Raising Your Children's Children: Help for Grandparents Raising Grandkids by Martha Evans Sparks

Self-Image

Search for Significance

My Utmost for His Highest by Oswald Chambers
Pilgrim's Progress by John Bunyan
Stomping Out the Darkness: Discover Your True Identity in Christ and Stop Putting Up with the World's Garbage by Neil T. Anderson and Dave Park
The Hiding Place by Corrie ten Boom
The Root of Rejection by Joyce Meyer
How to Succeed at Being Yourself by Joyce Meyer

Guilt and Shame

A Woman's Guide to Breaking Bondages by Quin Sherrer and Ruthanne Garlock

People Pleasing

Approval Addiction by Joyce Meyer

Boundaries

Boundaries by Dr. Henry Cloud and Dr. John Townsend
Safe People and Boundaries by Dr. Henry Cloud

The Word vs. the World

Fool's Gold?: Discerning Truth in an Age of Error by John MacArthur

Financial Matters

Living on a Budget

How to Manage Your Money by Larry Burkett
Taming the Money Monster by Ron Blue
The Complete Financial Guide for Young Couples by Larry Burkett
The Total Money Makeover by Dave Ramsey
Your Finances in Changing Times by Larry Burkett

Career Choices

Middle-Class Lifeboat: Careers and Life Choices for Navigating a Changing Economy by Paul and Sarah Edwards
Jesus, Career Counselor: How to Find (and Keep) Your Perfect Work by Laurie Beth Jones

Training Your Children in Finances

Three Cups: A Lesson in Life and Money for Children by Tony Townsley and Mark St. Germain

The Ability to Create Wealth

More Than Enough: 10 Keys to Changing Your Financial Destiny by Dave Ramsey

ACKNOWLEDGMENTS

All glory to God for His love for me and mankind. I feel honored to pen these words to help others live an abundant life and fulfill their kingdom dream as they live right according to the Word.

To my husband, José, for loving me through the long days and late nights of completing this project; and for demonstrating tenacity by finishing two books while I was still in process. I thank him for holding me together through three computer crashes and buying me a new laptop to get the job done.

To my mother, Adell B. Dickinson, an example of godliness and holiness, my friend, confidante, partner in the gospel, travel buddy, sounding board, cheerleader, and voice of reason. Thanks for the late nights of laughter and support. To my dad, Deacon Clyde Dickinson, for his wit and wisdom, as well as helping me to stay on task.

To my brother André for help in the recovery process when I lost files on three separate occasions. Ouch.

To Pamela Hudson for her friendship and partnership in the gospel for the past twenty years. Thanks for walking with me through this project and many others.

To Brenda Lester (and Pastor Bonner for recommending her) for helping to review and edit the early phases of the project and Tracey Frazier for helping review and edit the latter phase.

To the ladies at the Table of Eight (Kim Davis, Jan Newby, Dr. Lisa Fuller, Rev. Georgia Hill, Nicoela Terrell, Colleen Holbrook, Yvonne Hill, Tracey Frazier); the Magnificent Haiti Team of Eight (especially Judy Richardson); my Detroit Bible Institute counseling students; and all the others who had to listen to me talk about the book and who submitted ideas for the book.

To my Evangel Clergy family (especially Pastor Christopher and Minister Yodit Brooks, Pastors Phil and Renee Carr, Minister Rhonda Smith, Minister Sandra Parker).

To Marilyn White and the staff of *Precious Times* magazine, where some of the situations and scenarios first appeared in the quarterly publication. To all of the women who have written in seeking godly counsel and whose lives have been impacted by these words.

To Matt Parker, my longtime mentor and friend (for over twenty-five years). Thanks for believing in me, opening doors of opportunity, and setting the example of how to enter in and take others with me.

Thank God for the staff at RBC: To Mart and Rick De-Haan, Carol Holquist, and Bill Crowder for coming to visit me in Southfield. Thanks to Judy, Miranda, Carol, and the DHP staff for hosting me and Mother on our trips to Grand Rapids and for introducing me to Graeters. What a nice treat for each step of progress. Your patience, affirming nature, and guidance were greatly appreciated.

To my new family and home at RBC for all the love, support, encouragement, and new open doors to impact the kingdom of God.